MW01235213

The Authentic You

The Authentic You

Josie Slaton Terry

BALBOA
PRESS

A DIVISION OF HAY HOUSE

Copyright © 2013 Josie Slaton Terry.

All rights reserved. No part of this book may be used or reproduced by
any means, graphic, electronic, or mechanical, including photocopying,
recording, taping or by any information storage retrieval system
without the written permission of the publisher except in the case
of brief quotations embodied in critical articles and reviews.

www.josieslatonterry.com
Photo by Shawn Brooks
www.shawnbrooksphotography.com
Cover Design by: www.shawnbrooksdesign.com

Balboa Press books may be ordered through booksellers or by contacting:

Balboa Press
A Division of Hay House
1663 Liberty Drive
Bloomington, IN 47403
www.balboapress.com
1-(877) 407-4847

Because of the dynamic nature of the Internet, any web addresses or
links contained in this book may have changed since publication and
may no longer be valid. The views expressed in this work are solely those
of the author and do not necessarily reflect the views of the publisher,
and the publisher hereby disclaims any responsibility for them.

The author of this book does not dispense medical advice or prescribe the use
of any technique as a form of treatment for physical, emotional, or medical
problems without the advice of a physician, either directly or indirectly. The
intent of the author is only to offer information of a general nature to help you
in your quest for emotional and spiritual well-being. In the event you use any
of the information in this book for yourself, which is your constitutional right,
the author and the publisher assume no responsibility for your actions.

Any people depicted in stock imagery provided by Thinkstock are models,
and such images are being used for illustrative purposes only.
Certain stock imagery © Thinkstock.

Printed in the United States of America.

ISBN: 978-1-4525-7943-6 (sc)
ISBN: 978-1-4525-7944-3 (e)

Balboa Press rev. date: 11/14/2013

Ships Are Safe In The Harbour

All I live for is now
All I stand for is where and how
All I wish for are magic moments

As I sail through change
My resolve remains the same
What I chose are magic moments

Because ships are safe in the harbour
But that is not what ships are made for
The mind could stretch much further
But it seems that is not what our minds are trained for

We call for random order
You can't control Mother nature's daughter

Ships are safe in the harbour
But that is not what ships are built for
The witch hunter roams
The scary thing is that he's not alone
He's trying to down my magic moments

As we sail through change
Ride the wind of a silent rage
And sing laments of magic moments

(Author unknown)

Dedication

To the memories of my parents:

Marvin and Josephine Slaton

Acknowledgements

When my first book, *Fabulous Over Forty* was published my family and friends celebrated with me. I felt like a mother hearing the words "you have a pretty baby". Blessings to all for every book that was purchased! Thank you again and again for sharing my dream with me. But, it's not over. I am adding to the list. If you liked *Fabulous Over Forty* you will absolutely love *The Authentic You!*

My parents, Marvin and Josephine Slaton certified me as a child with the encouragement to dream big. I felt like I was handpicked (as with my other siblings) to live my *authentic* life. They taught me to appreciate (without jealousy) the successes of other big dreamers. They molded my pathway from childhood to adulthood with many life's lessons:

- Be a loving and kind person.
- Trust in God.
- Treat others with respect.
- The right friends are vital.
- Realize all things are possible if you believe.
- Don't cry over spilled milk … just buy more.

- and their favorite lesson — Hard work will not kill you.

I was taught well by my parents, and they knew that all *authentic* dreamers must have guidelines to support their calling through life.

This book is to acknowledge the *authentic* seekers both past and present; those who lived their true purpose and those who are now living their true purpose. It will motivate the a*uthentic* you into the refocus of your passion. Moreover, it will awaken you to recognize (and to avoid) the traps attempting to prevent you from your *authentic* life's calling. There have been great singers, actors, teachers, writers, and the list goes on, who cheated the world of their gifts because they said, "The road was too challenging and the sacrifice was too costly." On the other hand, there are dreamers who pressed on. People laughed at them and called their dream unrealistic; yet, they believed in their own dream and it paid off. Some dreamers were penniless and had no social life, but they held onto unwavering faith and waited (not knowing how or when) for the dream to come true. Through hell and high water "the dream made it".

When you hear a beautiful song, see a great movie, read a good book, wear a nice outfit, witness an amazing talent or gift in the world, just know someone paved the way with relentless endurance to live their *authentic* life. The *authentic* dreamers …are hereby acknowledged. *"I challenge you to be dreamers; I challenge you to be doers and let us make the greatest place in the world even better."* ~Brian Schweitzer

Introduction

The Persuaders' (1970 hit song) *Thin Line Between Love and Hate* are the exact words for me to properly introduce this book, because there is only a thin-line between the successful and unsuccessful. The successful people are more attentive to their purpose by reprogramming their mind to live their dreams "through hell and high water". This book will awaken "the *authentic* you" by giving you a glance into the lives of other *authentic* dreamers, while inspiring you to proclaim, "If they can do it — I can do it too!"

Table of Contents

Dream On

Chapter 1:

Everyone has a purpose from the dishwasher to the CEO of the company. Helping someone to birth a dream does not mean you have missed your purpose. All *authentic* leaders need *authentic* supporters, partners, and cheerleaders in their corner. Life is about finding your position and serving that position wholeheartedly. When everyone on the bus is in support of the dream... the dream will overflow and bless the village.

The mission. — Three years after writing my first book, *Fabulous Over Forty* my faithful followers asked, "When will your next book be published?" Did they know (at that particular time) they were speaking prophetically? This book began to burn in my soul; however, I wasn't shouting "Hallelujah!" Writing takes time and energy. As with my first book, the dream won and (knowing me) I wasn't going to quietly let this dream die. There I was again preparing my mind and body for a new mission (writing this book). Like a soldier prepares for battle, I put on my gear. As simple as it may sound or look, birthing a dream is not easy. But as a mother would say after giving birth "having the baby is more rewarding than the pain."

Adrienne Prather – My brilliant young friend Adrienne Prather overcame her shyness and personal heartaches through writing beautiful poems. One of my favorite is *Dream on Dreamer.* In the poem she says, *"Your dreams are not impossible, you are not dead."* Pondering over my new writing mission I asked my soul, "What are you saying to me? I knew my loyalty of being all that I could be, accomplishing my unfulfilled dreams, and helping others (to do the same) were important concerns for me. My subconscious sent a tweet to me about living the *authentic* life "strong and prosperous". Writing about the life "we" were born to live became my mission. As I previously mentioned, writing takes time, energy, and focus; yet at the same time it provides me with motivation that I'm willing to share with each of you. The clock on the wall was saying "it's time" to live your dreams. Nature was proclaiming "this is the season" for the dreamers to arise and shine. Paraphrasing Adrienne's poem, "We are not dead... Dream on Dreamer." Oliver Wendell Holmes a great writer was quoted saying, *Many people die with their music still in them. Why is this so? Too often it is because they are always getting ready to live. Before they know it, time runs out."*

The Journey of the dream. – Some dreamers start living their purpose early in life: professional singers, writers, dancers, speakers, actors and so on. They had good leadership steering them along the way. However, studies show that the majority of them discover their purpose (*authentic* self) later in life's journey after facing trials and tribulations. The point of this book is "early or late" the dreamers and their dreams have a reason and a season; and the journey of living with purpose "rocks with authenticity".

The dream starts with the first step. – During my studies of many biographies for this book and for my personal encouragement, I realized that once you open the vault of your heart a passion and yearning for the dream develops inside of you. Poet, Rainer Maria Rilke said, *"The only journey is the one within."* With that said, the way to the dream is in the understanding of your true self. The dream (for you) will become your lover, as in the movie *Strange Bedfellows* (1965); the dream fires up a romance between the present you and your *authentic* self — producing the life you were born to live. You can't start the journey until you take the first step. To birth the dream inside of you, you must step out, reach out and never stop dreaming (bigger).

The second step. — The way to not lose your dream (while experiencing problems in life) is by becoming an eyewitness of other *authentic* dreamers. Watch how they overcome hardships. Take notes on how they maintain strong faith in the struggle. Moreover, know that right now (not tomorrow) is your time to recharge your passion. Believe that life's problems are not happening to you; instead, life's problems are happening so you may develop into your *authentic* self.

The third step. — Live your life free of blame. If you fail...start again. If you fall...start again. If you mess up... start again. Failure is not an option. As stated in a popular song by Donnie McClurkin "We fall down but we get up... again." The third step summary: While making plans for your dreams do not allow mistakes to stop you! Be your *authentic* self and refuse to live in condemnation.

Your day is coming. — There is an old hymn my mother used to sing that says, "There's another day coming and I'm glad about it." For every *authentic* dreamer your day is coming so be glad about it. Right now it may look "gloom and doom", but stay true to the mission of your dream. Keep the passion burning inside, and know with faith a miracle can happen when you least expect it. Life wasn't meant to be wasted – be unstoppable. Television host, actor, and comedian Arsenio Hall said in an interview, *"No one expected me to succeed",* but proving the naysayers wrong he succeeded anyway and became his *authentic* self. Live your life (so brightly) so that others can find their dreams from the rays of your light. *"The journey of a thousand miles begins with one step."* ~Lao Tzu

Don't let the dream die. — You will win some races and lose some battles, but you can't quit! Find your second-wind to keep going, because the finish-line is so close. In the midst of being my most "fabulous self", and after the celebration of my first book, I got stuck in the day to day challenges, and lost my motivation to dream. My parents died, my business experienced financial hardships, and I got involved with dishonest people who tried to take legal action against me. I started believing the stories of sadness, hurt and lack as my life's journey. I didn't know if I would ever write another book. Nonetheless, I got up and fed myself daily with good motivation, as well as surrounded myself with the right people (my remedies to start dreaming again). Wilma Rudolph (the first American female runner to win three gold medals at a single Olympics) said, *"Never underestimate the power of dreams and the influence of the human spirit."*

Your dream is speaking. — Be ready to hear your dream speak to you in the strangest places and at the oddest times. It could be while you're at work, in the grocery store, riding the bus, driving your car, or even when you're in the shower.

My dream announced its timing to me during a "mix and mingle" networking function. I was there with a few of my "fabulous over forty" friends enjoying an especially pleasant evening (I was content promoting my first book). All at once after three years, I felt a whisper in my spirit "you don't have time to keep smelling this coffee". That night, the new dream began to call me by name and I became restless in Georgia. The awareness of this book made the room stand still and I became engaged in a serious conversation with my thoughts. I tried to dismiss these thoughts because I knew (from the first book) the level of dedication this dream required of me. I tried to fight the thoughts so they would disappear; but they were relentless and intensified. That night the journey of writing *The Authentic You* began. Honestly, I could not put the thoughts of writing this book behind me for fear of having unfulfilled dreams to follow me for the rest of my life.

Marie Simpson — My friend Marie Simpson reinvented herself, and she didn't do a lot of talking about it. She had a desire to live her dreams —so she just did it. At one time, Marie was a private and reserved person who worked in corporate America. She did a complete turnaround; she left corporate America, moved to a new city, and worked on President Obama's 2009 campaign. When I caught up with Marie, she was living her *authentic* life. She looked younger and happier. She said laughingly, "One door opened another door, and life just became an adventure." Today, Marie teaches workshops helping others to have a better life through meditation. She really thinks outside of the box. Keep in mind that if the journey is too bumpy or if you feel that you've lost your way, simply do as a GPS tracking device instructs and "Recalculate".

Shakti Gawain — A pioneer in the field of personal development, Shakti Gawain's biography says she has written numerous best-selling books on personal development. Yet, there was a time when she sat on her dreams before receiving a push from someone close to her (everyone needs supportive friends). I read that her books sold over 10 million copies and were translated into more than 30 languages. Shakti's biography states that for over 25 years she has raised awareness and developed balance and wholeness in the lives of many. She is the co-founder of a publishing company and has appeared on Oprah...enough said. I emailed Shakti to let her know how much her story intrigued me and I received a courteous email in return. She is definitely an achiever of her dreams and that is *authentic.* *"Make contact with your inner Child, your Mentor within,"* advises Shakti. *"That teacher knows which fork in the road to follow. And you know when you have chosen right, because then you feel alive."* ~Shakti Gawain

Danny DeVito — A dreamer's day is coming. Actor Danny DeVito said in one of his interviews that he was rejected by a casting director because of his height, but he didn't let the rejection stop him from becoming one of Hollywood's heavyweights. In fact, his height was a part of his *authentic* purpose. He didn't allow others to define him, and his height could not stop him from becoming an actor, comedian, director, producer and a successful person.

Keep your determination. — "Success doesn't know height, race, age, gender or education — success knows determination." You will hear these words declared in this book over and over again because no one can steal your success story. Although they may steal your credit cards or personal identification, they cannot steal or take away your dream. The way you look, walk and talk are the origins for your purpose. When God told Moses to go and speak to Pharaoh regarding the children of Israel's freedom from Egypt (bondage), Moses told God that he wasn't a good speaker (paraphrasing). God replied to Moses, "Who has made man's mouth?" You must realize that you are completely outfitted for your dream. As with Danny DeVito use what you (already) have.

Think outside the box. — Composer and violinist Fritz Kreisler told the story of a fan who excitedly ran up to him after one of his concerts and said, *"I would give my whole life to play as beautifully as you do."* Kreisler replied, *"I did!"* Successful *authentic* people will do what others put off doing; like my friend Marie, they think outside of the box:

1. Go online and research subjects related to your dream to obtain more knowledge.

2. Check out networking sites and locate dreamers of like passion.

3. Do a vision board and mentally see yourself living your dream.

Dream the fear away. − I met Jan, a customer and now friend, while working with her on a business transaction. She told me that she was unable to fulfill her true dream of being a professional singer because she couldn't stomach standing in front of a crowd. She had severe stage fright. I asked her, "Do you really think other famous singers didn't experience some degree of stage fright?" When you think you are the only one feeling fearful about a dream, you are mistaken. Successful people do what they have to do, fear or no fear. The French Philosopher, Michel de Montaigne said, *"There is no passion as contagious as that of fear."* I advised Jan to write a daily confession to recite; seeing the dream bigger than the fear. Everyone experience and overcome some form of fear. Don't allow fear to block your destiny so "walk in faith and not in fear".

The Other You

Chapter 2:

When you attempt to understand life "better" this is what you will discover...the other you. The person you question in the mirror (of your heart) is your other self "aka" the real you. The other you is also known as the other-self; this is where you'll find your life's purpose (the *authentic* you). Did you play "make-believe when you were a child?" Did you ever live in a fantasy world to escape the things you didn't like? Most people have, but if you want to live a victorious life you must put away the make-believe mindset. In other words the Bible declares, *"You have to put away your childish ways."* Now is the time to discover the other you...the *authentic* you. I heard a story about a woman who lived her life daydreaming, which is not to be confused with living your dreams. She didn't dream with a purpose; instead, she often said, "Let's make-believe ..." Her life remained the same because it lacked substance to manifest her dream. For the most part, movies are composed of people who were hired to portray the character of somebody else. The real world must be cared for with dreams that are *authentic.* Actor Morris Chestnut said, *"This industry is very make-believe and you're caught in a false sense of what reality is."*

Do your work. - Just because you do things in a different way doesn't mean you are crazy. The dreamers that others called crazy are (for the most part) the successful entrepreneurs in the world today. It's a day by day journey of facing the obstacles that are trying to keep you from your *authentic* life. Spiritual teacher, author and television personality Iyanla Vanzant expresses it as *"doing your work."* Steps for ushering in your other powerful self are as follows:

1. Taking time to hear your passion speak.
2. Getting professional counseling for unresolved hurts.
3. Developing an uncomplaining spirit as you wait on your season.

The transformation. — The *authentic* life brings out the real person; transforming an accountant into a comedian, or the shy withdrawn office clerk into a famous entertainer. Birthing into your purpose, the wall-flower becomes a party planner, the skinny-weakling is now a heavyweight boxer, and the person who was considered unattractive is now a supermodel. Just like prayer changes things, success transforms people. *"All successful people men and women are big dreamers. They imagine what their future could be, ideal in every respect, and then they work every day toward their distant vision, that goal or purpose."* ~Brian Tracy

You have what it takes. – You cannot compare yourself to others; you must develop your gift within. You have what it takes to be the best you. You can (and should) live your dreams! The older you get you'll either have a drive to further develop yourself, or you'll get lazy and say "forget about it". It will take willpower to get up and get going. God is with you and there are so many options to increase your self-discipline, and to give your will-power a boost such as: prayer, meditation, laughter, taking a vacation, learning a new dance, listening to music, exercising and preparing good meals. When you are eager for change, you'll get past the fear of change and start the campaign of change. You CAN prepare yourself and get ready to experience the dream of your life. *"Stay focused, go after your dreams and keep moving toward your goals."* ~LL Cool J

You are the treasure in the chest. – Life is not like a pizza with all the slices in place. You may have had too many bites, hits and heartaches to deal with. There are times when you don't know who you are. Like the computer you need to refresh. You must understand how the mistakes, hurts, rejections, losses, and heartaches not only hurt, but they are also shaping you for your other self (the *authentic* you). There are commercials saying, "You have unclaimed money." Well, you may not have any unclaimed money, but you do have an "unclaimed life" to live. Like a pirate searching for hidden treasure search your heart for your dreams. Use every trial as a stepping-stone to push you toward your *authentic* self. No mountain is too high to reach your goal, because your *authentic* self is established in the climb. James Allen, author of *"As a Man Thinketh"* says, *"Circumstance does not make the man; it reveals him to himself."*

Be who "your dreams say you are". - Typically, everyone wants to be the person who they say they are. But who are you without titles, positions, possessions or relationships? What happens when life gives you a giant test, the marriage is over, the kids are away at college and old friends are not around? What happens when the party is over and you go home alone? What happens when the person you love doesn't love you? Who is the real person in the mirror? Does the person in the mirror love you? How do you define yourself when you do not have the props? Have you discovered YOU? So many questions to answer, but guess what? You are not alone; there is a crossroad in every person's life. Many times the questions are never answered, because the truth hurts.

Benjamin Franklin said, *"Those things that hurt, instruct."* The truth stops hurting (or doesn't hurt as much) once you are living the life of your dream and purpose.

Don't allow the questions to stop you. - Famous people are no different from you. Fantasia, an American Idol winner, sings in one of her songs, "Sometimes you got to lose before you can win." Famous people did not succeed because it was easier; they succeeded because they didn't allow the questions to stop them:

- First, analyze where you are and how you got there.
- Next, link with the right friends or support network.
- Take time to "ask and answer" the questions hindering your progress.
- Don't settle − make the change.
- Be determined to be an *authentic* "high achiever!"

"High achievers spot rich opportunities swiftly, make big decisions quickly and move into action immediately. Follow these principles and you can make your dreams come true." ~Robert H. Schuller

Under construction. - The construction site does not look like the beautiful high rise building it was designed to be;

but as the builders continue working on it, it will eventually become a stunning tower. Just as you continue to grow in the challenges of life; you may not look like it, but you are coming into your purpose. Standing strong in the trials prepares you to bulldoze the old you "out" and the new you "in". Your construction signs should read: "Finally, I am living my *authentic* dream."

Avoid distractions. – There is a story about Chemist and Inventor Marvin Pipkin, who would not allow others to discourage him from his work. He found a way to frost the inside of the bulb with acid (to strengthen each bulb). As a new chemist, he had to refuse discouragement from others and he did what was in his heart to complete his invention. The distraction of others will be there, but it's a part of the construction; dealing with doubters and those with bad tempers can lead to mental discouragement. You must keep the main thing — the main thing. Some people are not a part of your dream. For this reason, your conversation with them must be limited because they can side-track you, and waste the time you'll need for your dream. Keep focused and do what is needed to become your accomplished self. *"First say to yourself what you would be; and then do what you have to do."* ~Epictetus

Your real life. - An actor in touch with his or her *authentic* self knows where the performance starts, and when the curtain closes…that's the end. The real life person leaves the stage and the pretended character stays in the theater. One day I heard someone say, "You take pictures of your family to the office, but you don't take pictures of your office home." Like the lady in an earlier chapter who lost her dream in "make-believe"; if you live a "make-believe" life day and night, you'll soon lose touch with reality. It all starts looking the same and that's when you find yourself "believing you are someone else" and the *authentic* self is not able to exist. Make-believe can cross over into romances and leave its victims with a broken-heart; because it turns out they were in love with a stranger. If you stay true to who you are, you will be able to see the signs of the pretenders. To say this short and sweet "live your real life" and get off the merry-go-round of make-believe. The real you cannot blossom forth until the fake you cease to exist. You have both the capacity and the obligation to be your bon-a-fide self. *"You must take the first step. The first steps will take some effort, maybe pain. But after that, everything that has to be done is real-life movement."* ~Ben Stein

Trania Jones - I was talking with my friend Trania Jones, a powerful conference organizer. On this particular day she was not happy with the progress of her conferences; feeling the need to do more. As we talked, I thought about how the conferences empowered the audience. I told her with great excitement, "You have a 'T.D. Jakes' Woman Thou Art Loose assignment on your life!" As I shared with her about the preparation of timing for a dream to develop she got the picture. The conversation ignited her faith to see that her dream was bigger than she could "dare ask or think".

Recognize the BBW. — In the process of becoming the *"authentic you"* you will have those "ups" and "downs" thoughts, but just know those thoughts can change. You must keep yourself motivated and act in-line with the truth of your purpose. Recognize the BBW (Big Bad Wolf). It is full of many negative thoughts: "You're not good enough", "you're not attractive enough", and "you're not smart enough". The BBW has no mercy picking on children and adults. It never stops "you can't do it", "you'll never have it", "it's too late", or "you messed up big –time". Eagerly some media, family members, and friends agree with the BBW and live in negativity. They are looking for victims to join them. If you stop and entertain them you will hear "you know it's impossible to have a new home or job in this kind of economy", "you are too old to go back to school", "it's hard to find someone suitable to date", "look to be sick with this cold weather", and the all-time favorite "life is just too hard". If you fill yourself with positive words, then the negative words of the BBW will not stop you. Reverse all the negativity coming at you by asking yourself, "Is anything too hard for God?"

Use your time wisely. - You can't connect with everyone so ... don't try. Some people wake-up crazy. While you are singing "praises to God" they are cussing and fussing at the cat. Beware of them and do not get into their negative mindset ... by trying to figure them out. You know them: they are the thoughtless drivers on the road, the nasty store clerks, and the unfriendly neighbors. Don't let these kinds of people poison your positive vision on life. They are not going where you are going. They are also the ones jealous because they see the blessing you are about to receive. They hurt you, but make you feel like they are the victim. Control your time around them, because you can't get back the valuable time lost. Use your time wisely and stay on your mission. *"We must use time wisely and forever realize that the time is always ripe to do right."* ~Nelson Mandela

Authentic people are free-spirited. - The songs of singer, songwriter and record producer, Robert Sylvester Kelly (better known as R. Kelly) surpassed all of his bad press, because his message captivates the listeners, and become as his hit song, *"Happy People"*. Recorded in 2005 "Happy People"

is R. Kelly's feel good and timeless dance song. Another timeless feel good song is by musician and songwriter Bobby McFerrin. This immediate Billboard hit, "Don't Worry, Be Happy" brought him worldwide recognition. His song confirms you don't have to worry, just be and stay happy. Worrying over your life will not change it. *Authentic* people live in happiness through nature, beautiful sceneries, lovely paintings, and of course the gift of music.

Authentic people live, love and make life fun. — On the road to success happy people know that a happy heart is medicine for their soul. They look at the opportunity in every situation. For example: They may lose their job, but at the same time they see "a new career opportunity coming open". On the other hand, unhappy people are only happy for a short period of time. They look for misery like they are looking for gold and find comfort in it. Unhappy people want everyone to know how bad things are. Dreamers have to move on from them. Unhappy people remind me of the song by country music artist Tracy Byrd, *When Mama Ain't Happy, Ain't Nobody Happy.*

You are God's gift. – I was told that after being rejected by their childhood love, some pretty girls believe they are not pretty and some attractive guys lose their confidence. If you add living in a dysfunctional household to the story, the outcome will have them not believing in their full potential. The work must be done: "healing the past with forgiveness", "transforming negative thoughts to positive thoughts", and "renewing the mind from impossible to possible." Louise Hay, founder of Hay House Radio and Publishing Company said to do the mirror exercise, whereby you look into the mirror and confirm positive things to yourself: You are God's gift to the world, you have a successful purpose in this life, expect the impossible, and expect double for your trouble. *"I find that when we really love and accept and approve of ourselves exactly as we are, then everything in life works."* ~Louise L. Hay

Robert Kiyosaki - In the book *Rich Dad Poor Dad* by Robert Kiyosaki and Sharon Lechter, there is a parable about two fathers: a rich father and a poor father. The rich dad taught his son about prosperity and gave him the thinking tools to live a rich life. The poor dad taught his son to accept a common lifestyle. You may not have rich earthly parents, but you can still live a rich and powerful life. You were taught to believe in a system that you can change, and that change starts in your thoughts. Reprogramming your thoughts can change your life. I talked with a new customer, who shared with me his desire to start his own business; however, he felt like he was too damaged from his childhood abuse to do a good job with the dream. His thoughts were defeating his purpose. So I said to him, "You have the choice of what you want to think, and the thoughts you give the most time to will become dominant". *"The size of your success is measured by the strength of your desire; the size of your dream; and how you handle disappointment along the way."* ~Robert Kiyosaki

Face your fear. — I know of a man who always talks about what he used to do, he lives on the merit of his past jobs. He talks about how good his old relationships were and subconsciously thinks those were his best years. He can't move on to a purposeful life because he has not faced his fear of the unknown. The fear of facing the future keeps him living in the past. The *authentic* you can't keep looking back and be successful. You do not have a spirit of fear. It was self-taught; there is freedom in truth. The bible says once you know the truth you are set free. The *authentic* dreamers soar with the spirit of freedom to accomplish greatness. *"I have learned over the years that when one's mind is made up, this diminishes fear; knowing what must be done does away with fear."* ~Rosa Parks

Fear of rejection. - A customer and friend came into my office feeling down and needing words of encouragement. At the time I was cleaning out some old files. As he talked, I listened and after his "misery loves company" talk I offered him a software disk that I was ready to trash. He asked, "Why are you giving me this disk?" I said, "Because I don't need it and I thought maybe you could use it." He asked, "What's on it?" I replied, "I don't know and whatever is on it is outdated, but you may have it." He reached out his hand and took it. Then I asked him, "Why did you take a disk you didn't need?" He replied, "Because you gave it to me." He had a fear of pleasing others while neglecting to express his true feelings. It took a moment to sink in but he got the point. You just can't let people unload their trash on you. Meet the opposition face-to-face, and facing the fear of rejection will stop it. *"A rejection is nothing more than a necessary step in the pursuit of success."* ~Bo Bennett

Footsteps of a dream. ~ Walking in your own steps means "being willing to walk with a different beat". Henry David Thoreau an American philosopher wrote, *"If a man loses pace with his companions, perhaps it is because he hears a different drummer. Let him step to the music which he hears however measures, or far away".* The person I most admire for living his *authentic* life is Dr. Martin Luther King, Jr. In his famous speech he talked about walking to the beat of a different drummer. For this reason, we know Dr. King as a great leader. He changed the world with his life of service. He met the challenges before him and brought about a change;

his dream will be forever honored and recognized as our dream. He walked in the beat of his purpose. Walking to the beat of your purpose means knowing yourself. In my first book *Fabulous Over Forty* there is a sub-chapter entitled "Know Yourself". It reads: "Knowing yourself is a confidence booster. Aging well means identifying what turns you on and off. God designed your blueprint especially for you and you are an amazing individual. You have what it takes to change the world where you live. If you know yourself, you will also know who is right and wrong for your life. To be who you were meant to be, you must find the strength to know yourself."

Live in victory. - Appalling, but true; some (very smart) people are living in a prison of their own doing. They walk around in a lost daze, and they are mad with the world. They want everyone to pay for their misfortune. It was Abraham Lincoln who said, *"You can't help the poor by being one of them."* The only way to help people who (decided to) live unproductively is to lead by example: Learn strong points from other's success stories. Look for ways to increase YOU, and yearn for all life has to give. Refuse to live life in unhappiness. Become the powerful person you know you should be - dump hopelessness like a hot potato. Don't just talk success, be successful; be victorious and not a victim.

It's time to start declaring a new beginning over your life. Waking every day with a new freshness in mind and spirit, singing a new song with a smile on your face — even laughing with the birds outside of your window. The birds have no cares because they know God will take care of them. *"I count him braver who overcomes his desires than him who conquers his enemies; for the hardest victory is over self."* ~Aristotle

It's only an opinion. - When you come into your *authentic* self, people will always have an opinion about you; just ignore it. For example, I was at a social gathering and a certain woman began to give us her opinion regarding another woman. She said belittling things about this woman that could have formed a negative opinion of her in our minds. The things she said had nothing to do with the truth about this other woman's character. This is an example of what you come up against when you are around unauthentic people… their negative opinions. These kinds of people prefer to criticize rather than show support and give encouragement. Having a critical attitude gives them validation for not having a productive life (by their choice). Being your *authentic* self will not change someone's opinion of you. It's only an opinion and opinions are cheap.

The right friends. – Know who your true friends are; the *"authentic* you" cannot afford to have a Judas sitting at the table trying to get news to start and spread rumors. On the ladder of success you need friends who are *authentic.* Friends who will go the extra mile with you, and when times are hard they will not checkout. The old you built friendships with people who could not grow with you, but you know better now. It's not that you're dropping these friends; instead, it's you becoming your *authentic* self. You can help them once you help yourself. Find the friends who don't want to be you, but they want to be their best *authentic* self because of you. *"Lots of people want to ride with you in the limo, but what you want is someone who will take the bus with you when the limo breaks down."* ~Oprah Winfrey

You become your own HERO. – Once you set your mind to not quit, stop complaining or thinking negatively then no problem, no storm, no heartache will win over you. You are not here alone. The bible says, "God is always with you and closer than the breath you breathe." This truth must dwell in your heart and you must give life some time to work on your behalf. You were meant to have a strong and prosperous life: an overflowing life, a successful journey, love forevermore, peace that passes all understanding, joy unspeakable, goodness and continuous mercy. What more could you ask for? But it's not motivation alone that will produce results—it's your ability to not quit on yourself. Stay a persistent dreamer even when you don't feel motivated, and when you don't see the results — don't quit. Recently, I had to face some closed doors. I had to do what I am telling you:

1. Resist worry.
2. Keep a good attitude.
3. Get the right motivation.
4. Work the planned purpose.
5. Wait patiently for the outcome.
6. Believe that it will (ALL) work-out for the good.

You were born for opportunity. - Motivator speaker Les Brown says, *"You must be hungry,"* meaning hungry for your *authentic* self. Everyone wants a piece of the pie. There is enough to go around. I strongly promote "you'll get in life what you believe". It's in vain to sit back and feel helpless. From others' biographies, I've realize the ocean of opportunity is available, if you keep on—keeping on. You are not waiting on opportunity; opportunity is waiting on you to be prepared. Singer Norman Hutchins said it best in his song, *"God's Got A Blessing (With My/Your Name On It!)."* Get in line with what your "positive" spirit is saying to you and follow your heart.

The Ego trip. – You must stay alert to not lose your *authentic* (other) self in your success. Warning! You must protect your *authentic* calling from the ego trip, because it is a deadly ride, and the down fall of many success stories. Nevertheless, you hear it all the time about celebrities or other high profile persons who went astray because of the ego. They started out humble and *authentic,* but the success that was "meant for good" went wrong, and the ego took over. The traits of the ego: lack of love, lack of good will, and an obstructer of plans. Through understanding and applying wise principles you can get back on track.

Mary J. Blige — Be a person who makes a difference. The *authentic* person does not live for "my four and no more." The *authentic* person achieves success and goes back to the old neighborhood to help out; this person is a hero of positive change. I've never understood how a person could gain success yet not reach back to where they grew up; to renovate the playground, give back to the community center, or help influence the kids on the block to live a better life. That's what the *authentic* life is all about...getting to give back. Like Mary J. Blige who co-founded the Foundation for the Advancement of Women Now (FFAWN). I read where she became a mentor at an all girls' public high school in the Bronx, New York, where she is also providing scholarships for these students to attend college. There are others giving back and I thank God for them. They didn't forget. They are the real *authentic* people.

Vanessa L. Williams - I was in a conversation discussing the inner strength of a person when the conversation led to Vanessa L. Williams and the time she became the first African-American to be crowned Miss America. The pressure from the scandal, which caused her to relinquish her title early, was enough to give her a breakdown. It was amazing to see how Williams' showed strength and rebounded to build her career as an entertainer; earning Grammy, Emmy, and Tony Award nominations. Her accomplishments after Miss America have been quite astonishing. It pays not to quit —greater things develop. There was a time I occupied an office location where Nick the maintenance man worked. In his eighties he had so much strength. He outperformed the younger guys half his age, including my brother, Aaron (in his fifties at the time). I never saw a time when Nick did not have a kind word for you. This was Nick's character as an *authentic* person which kept him strong.

Donald Trump — Using past failures can be a guide to success. I respect how Donald Trump used his failures as stepping stones. He is a well-known successful business tycoon, author and television personality. It was an honor to have the opportunity to attend one of his workshops. The energy in the room was on a natural high. His team (assigned to facilitate the workshop) displayed the same successful energy as Mr. Trump. No matter how others may view Mr. Trump, agree or disagree with him, he is still proof that a person can be successful in their business, if they don't allow their failures to defeat them. Donald Trump turned his failures into success stories. Calvin Coolidge the 30TH President said, *"Nothing in the world can take the place of persistence."*

P.T. Barnum — I read about P.T. Barnum who was an American businessman, showman and entertainer. He was also known for being a scam artist and for promoting celebrated hoaxes. He went on to become the founder of the circus (known to everyone) "Ringling Bros and Barnum & Bailey Circus." Although P.T. Barnum was an author, publisher, philanthropist, and for some time a politician, he knew himself and lived the life planned for him. He said, *"I am a showman by profession...and all the gilding shall make nothing else of me."*

Follow Your Heart

Chapter 3:

Countless number of people started their career working
on jobs that were not a part of their purpose. There
are times when the pursuit of the heart's dream is put on
hold and other career paths are chosen for many reasons
(one major reason is the money – looking and feeling good).
Starting my career, I was included in that countless number
working on a job just for the money. However, without an
authentic purpose or goal, my work started working against
me (seldom feeling my best self). The burning desire to
live with purpose must be resurrected; once I began to
pursue my dream (my *authentic* calling), my life aligned
with better health and peace of mind. (In fact, this is the
reason you're reading this book). Life is about working
with purpose, seeing dreams coming true and living your
best *authentic* life. I read *Do What You Love The Money
Will Follow* by Marsha Sinetar and gained insight for living
purpose minded. Now is the time to live with vision and

intention! A timeless proverb says, *"Where there is no vision people perish."*

Dolores Hope — Success comes at any age. Dolores Hope, the wife of Bob Hope (actor and comedian) recorded her first album at the age of 83. She lived to be 102. It was around 1992 when Dolores Reade Hope recorded her first CD "Now and Then." After spending most of her life giving to others such as her husband, children, and a variety of charities, she took some time to do something for herself and performed for her fans. (Neither time, nor age can stop a dream from taking the stage). I read that Mrs. Hope recorded additional albums after the release of her first one. Dolores Reade Hope's undertaking speaks to the *authentic* person to keep dreaming, because the best is yet to come. Like Dolores Hope in her eighties, you can stun an entirely new generation with your gifts at any age.

Dale Carnegie — Decide to live in your purpose and set the pace for others to follow. Dale Carnegie's biography states how he was a poor farmer's boy. He managed to receive an education through his impoverish childhood, and after college he sold various products to make a living. He didn't quit on his dream to become a lecturer one day; he not only became a great lecturer, but also a successful writer. He developed the famous courses in self-improvement, salesmanship, corporate training, public speaking and interpersonal skills. These courses still exist many years later. (In fact, I attended a Dale Carnegie Training Seminar. It was uplifting and informative). Mr. Carnegie's life's work is still inspiring others to walk in their own power through many of his books to name a few: "How to Win Friends and Influence People" and "How to Stop Worrying and Start Living." The dominant themes of his books reflect on the possibilities of changing a persons' behavior by way of changing their reaction to life's situations. Dale Carnegie was poor and had limited resources when he started his journey; by turning his life around he left a legacy of positive and successful books. He proved that once you've weathered the storms, the blessings will overflow. That's *authentic! "Take a chance! All life is a chance. The man who goes farthest is generally the one who is willing to do and dare." *~Dale Carnegie

Andrew Carnegie — The biography of Andrew Carnegie (unrelated to Dale Carnegie) states that he immigrated to the United States as a child with his parents at a very early age. He worked hard as a factory worker and messenger boy only to become known as one of the most successful industrialist, businessman, entrepreneur and a major philanthropist in the world. He built Carnegie Steel Company, which later merged to create U.S. Steel. (My brother-in-law worked for

U.S. Steel; he was so proud of the job and the company). Andrew Carnegie is not only known for inspiring others to live successfully, he was also regarded as the second-richest man in history after John D. Rockefeller. He gave away most of his money to create many libraries, schools, and universities in the United States. Mr. Carnegie lived the rest of his life giving to charities. Mr. Carnegie was an *authentic* person. *"As I grow older, I pay less attention to what men say. I just watch what they do."* Andrew Carnegie

Napoleon Hill — "Think and Grow Rich" author, Napoleon Hill (inspired by Andrew Carnegie) books emphasize the power of personal thinking and the role it plays in personal success. Nearly every successful business person has read this book. Napoleon Hill was born in a one-room cabin. His mother died when he was nine years old. He started writing when he was thirteen. He knew his *authentic* calling was to write, he just needed the door of opportunity to open. He considered his interview of the industrialist Andrew Carnegie to be the turning point in his life. Napoleon Hill lived his *authentic* life and became known as one of the first producers of the modern kind of personal success books. The focal point of Hill's books (spoke about how achievement occurs) provide a formula of success for the average person. His book, "Think and Grow Rich", was published in 1937 and continues to be one of the best-selling books of all time. *"What the mind of man can conceive and believe, it can achieve"* is one of Hill's sealed expressions.

Wallace Wattles —Author, Wallace Wattles grew up in poverty, but later became wealthy. His book, "The Science of Getting Rich" explains how living and thinking a certain way makes one wealthy. It was a major inspiration for Rhonda Byrne's bestselling book and film "The Secret". I read in one of Wattles' biographies that he had little education. The thought crossed my mind, "how could a poor and uneducated man grow up to write about getting rich?" Wattles practiced the technique of creative visualization (the practice of seeking to affect the outer world via changing one's thoughts) — positive thinking. It is said that athletes use this technique to enhance their performance. This is also an immense way to enhance the *authentic* life: believing in your success before it happens.

Wake up to the real world. — I remember this guy who had a wonderful talent to fix any and everything. Nevertheless, he wouldn't listen. He had all the answers. He wouldn't face the abuse of his childhood or seek help for a sturdy standard of living. So, he stayed drunk. With all of the talent he had he never used it. He settled for the title…bum. It dismays me to see unused talent. While volunteering at a homeless shelter,

I met a lovely, but lonely lady who had a beautiful singing voice. I asked her about her life and she said, "I don't know what happened, I just lost my way in the bad and hard times of life." I encouraged her to know ... it's never too late to be your *authentic self.* The road to success has many detours; but it's important to remember, the road back to your destiny is still there. You eventually learn that detours are merely stepping stones. The wilderness is just one mile from the Promised Land. The person in the rubbish can live again. When you are one with your *authentic* self, you wake up to the real world! American founder of the Ford Motor Company, Henry Ford said, *"If you always do what you've always done, you'll get what you've always gotten."* If you don't settle for negative thinking then your life will change.

Keep moving forward. —You will face storms as you move forward, but like flowers growing from rain, this is a time of personal growth. Initially, starting my business turned out to mean working hours most of the time. The finances had its challenges and my family and social life were put on hold. Being the owner of my business meant turning off the lights, taking out the trash and being the last person to leave the office. Everyone told me that my first book should have been based on what I went through with my selection of employees. As I said, I've experienced moments when I wanted to go back to my old job because moving forward wasn't easy. Times got too hard. I asked myself, "Is this a dream or a nightmare?" But, I had to follow my heart. Moving forward and facing the trials grew me up. However, where you start does not mean it cannot and will not change. The lesson: Whether you start a business or work for someone else, the goal is to always stay in touch with your purpose, and keep moving forward.

Refresh yourself. — Gospel singer, Shirley Caesar's song, *"This Joy I have"* says you have some valuable things inside of you; joy, love and everything you need to have a complete life. People can't take your "God given" gifts from you, and lining up with your purpose has nothing to do with who likes you or what they say about you. Go beyond the naysayers and discover how to cultivate, promote, and live your real life. Discovering your *authentic* life should be on your "bucket list" and "things to do list". Make time for yourself, the best of you is always ahead of you:

- Set aside ME time.
- Start putting yourself first (from time to time).
- Relax, exhale and meditate.
- Eat healthy - keep a food diary (don't cheat),
- Exercise.

Protect your dream. — People will disappoint you. The bill collectors will overwhelm you, and you'll find yourself robbing "Peter to pay Paul". Don't get depressed; keep confessing "my breakthrough is coming". Keep working on your dream, start your daily confessions, keep a thankful heart, refresh your vision (write it down), and stay strong inside by listening to positive faith-filled messages. Protect the dream inside of you! Actor, John Travolta starred in the movie *The Boy in the Plastic Bubble*. The Plastic Bubble protected him from the germs of the outside world. You have to imagine yourself in a plastic bubble; avoiding the outside obstacles of life trying to prevent you from becoming your *authentic* self. Once coming into your *authentic* self the blessings received for all you have gone through will be worthy of the dream.

Take a chance on yourself — Norman Vincent Peale said, *"Every problem has in it the seeds of its own solution. If you don't have any problems, you don't get any seeds."* My true career started by following my heart and letting go of the rear view mirror wanting to retreat and go back. Yes, eventually I gave up the good paying job in accounting, and went back to school to study graphic design. The budget got tight and the pleasure of shopping was put on hold. Learning how to live on less was satisfied in the dream. However, I had to help the dream live, so I did what was needed, like taking part-time jobs to stay afloat. After completing art school, I worked some freelance jobs — and some were (really) free labor for the needed experience. My dream of working in alignment to my true self was in full collaboration to keep going. My first job as a graphic designer was with an advertising company. My paycheck was half of what I made at the accounting job, but it read: *Josie Slaton Terry, Graphic Designer.* Something inside of me registered. I went outside and looked up at the big blue sky, for which I could now see and appreciate. Loudly and happily I screamed, "Thank you God!" At that moment I knew how it felt to find myself; a piece of my life's puzzle was put into place. I did what every *authentic* person does "I took a chance on me". That day was one of the steps to this day, whereby I am known as, *author, Josie Slaton Terry.*

Rags (The Old You) / Riches (The Real You)

Chapter 4:

I can't say this enough … I love biographies! I love hearing about how someone at the bottom ascended to the top. I believe life is preordained for the "whosoever-will" to live in the overflowing goodness of God's blessings. The "whosoever-will" is the person who believes in the impossible becoming possible. Bishop T.D. Jakes compared the "Whosoever-will to a blank check." To me, that means "whosoever-will" can write the amount (on their dream-check) for as much as they are able to believe. When you can't see your way through the darkness in life, you need to be around faith builders, the people who provide the "how to" as a road map. As I mentioned in a previous chapter, "that's how success works; you learn from the successes of others". Martin H. Fischer said it this way, *"The world is your school."*

Live a thought out life. — Your life can change from poverty to wealth and from obscurity to fame overnight. You hear those stories all the time (from rags to riches stories). One day you are in the lost and found area of life and the next day "everybody knows your name." It's heartbreaking when someone thinks his or her life has no purpose and drift through life aimlessly. In the smallest deed there is purpose: helping a person to read, learning a new language, driving a car, or consoling someone during a tragedy. Most dreams begin with the small thought "maybe", and from there "I can", and from there "I will". With faith and work the dream starts to take shape and things change from bad to good. You must rid your thoughts of "poor me" and start thinking thoughts of goodwill. In the process of writing this book I had to attend a cousin's funeral. We grew up in the same hometown. Now he is dead at 57 years old. I grieved thinking, "Did he ever want more?" I was told when he became ill he said, "The pain is too much to bear." But as I observed the situation, it wasn't just the pain in his body; it was the pain of not living his real life. I felt like he gave up a long time ago or perhaps he never found the path for his life. Again, I wondered, "Did he ever want more in life" or better yet "Did he have hope for a better future?" I couldn't answer these questions. I just wanted to stay strong and focused. Keep in mind there are times when life appears to be too hard to bear, and it becomes confusing; but I know if you keep your thoughts strong and fruitful, the storms will surely pass, and your dream will survive.

Understand your season. — Living a life of purpose means having a full understanding of your season and not participating in worry or confusion. Wrong thinking and bad advice will cost you time and misguided purpose, and will have you feeling pressured and discouraged. You will think that you're off schedule with your life because of wrong thoughts whispering in your ear. Now you're in a hurry to be married, you have an issue with the job, or maybe the new home isn't available yet. Wrong thinking and receiving bad advice can cause you to start feeling left-out and out of touch with your journey. Control yourself, stop stressing and get in a spirit of "praise and thanksgiving". It's vital to understand that blessings are harvested by seasons:

1. The right time … we live by earth's calendar, but the universe has a calendar too. When things are scheduled to happen for you — they will take place at a set-time based on your readiness. Readiness means operating in the faith and focus of your purpose.

2. The right person… a relationship out of its season can generate a truckload of problems. In the right season you will have the right person in your life.

The time span it took for the right person to arrive in your life broke the bad patterns for the wrong person, who would hinder your *authentic* life.

3. The right job…a door must close before another door can open. It may feel like rejection, but it's not. The process will give you strength and a testimony of endurance.

4. The location…the home or the move may need some adjustments, but when it's your time all the doors and windows will open.

The "old you" didn't have the patience to wait, but the "new you" is willing and ready for the green light. The way to identify the "old you" and the "new you" will be based on your choices. The "old you" never learned from past mistakes; therefore, the mistakes were repeated. However, the "new you" was tired of the same awful relationships and bad opportunities, as a result, the "new you" made the leap and changed the old thought patterns that would tempt you to try and force open the wrong doors. In your season "you will not be delayed or denied". In the meantime, keep your faith strong and be ready for your season. *"Time is the wisest counselor of all."* ~Pericles

Develop A Hunger For Life. — When I moved to Atlanta, Georgia, from my small hometown of Woodbury, Georgia (population of 3,000 or less), I was in awe of the city life. Even though I was lonely and longed for my family and friends, I knew Atlanta (a one-hour drive from my hometown - a distant land for me) was the ticket to my dreams coming true. In spite of being homesick and struggling financially, there were opportunities for the life I longed to live. The only connection from my hometown to Atlanta was my Aunt Bell. However, the last thing she wanted was family members moving in with her. She agreed to give me six months to find my own place. Fully aware of her time restriction I hoped my shining personality, hard-work, and my determination to succeed would delay the six-month limit. But, at the end of the six months, she proved to be a woman of her word and released me. In other words, she gave me my walking papers. No mercy. It was approaching the night before Christmas, and there I was attending college, working part-time at a boutique and soon to be homeless. What was I to do?

The new you must be hungry for the dream. – I had a hunger to survive. Moving to Atlanta put me in touch with the "new/*authentic* me", but my aunt wanted me to leave. I knew I could go back home to "open arms", but the development into the person "I was called to be" would be put on-hold or lost. The next day at school, one of my friends told me about her mother's friend who had a room for rent. She was my saving grace and the rest is history. The spirit that never gives up will open doors and windows, when you least expect it. The story of my Aunt Bell was not over. I still loved her and in her later years of sickness, I was there for her until she left this life in her eighties. I was always so thankful she gave me the six months. It opened the door and allowed me to move from my hometown to Atlanta and through it all – I made it and the new person prevailed!

Be an over-comer. — When things look bad, as they sometimes will, you just can't stop. The next moment could be your breakthrough. The next call could be the life changing message. The next relationship could be the right one. But, you have to stay alert and understand your season. Every day is new, and life will be what you make it. As I read various biographies to draw encouragement for this book, I felt my mind expanding to the amazing stories of triumph. Each one left me with the words, "It's possible!" *"A man's gift maketh room for him, and bringeth him before great men."* ~Proverbs 18:16

Hillman Toombs, Esq. – My friend, Attorney Hillman Toombs and his wife Teresa are so dear to me. In the early days before starting his law practice, Mr. Toombs shared with me how he worked his way through law school. There were times when he was behind the grill and sold barbeque in his hometown of Columbus, Georgia. He used what he had and did what he had to do, while climbing the ladder of success to his *authentic* self. Today, he's a successful attorney in Riverdale, Georgia. If you feel a calling in your life to do more than you are presently doing, learn this lesson from Attorney Toombs: use what you are presently doing as plan "A" to get to plan "B". Don't curse the hand that is feeding you and paying the bills. Be creative. It may take time, but you will still get there.

Tina Turner — An *Authentic* Trailblazer. Singer and actress Tina Turner's family were share-croppers. Although she grew up poor, at the age of 16, she was determined to enter this new world of *Rhythm and Blues*. Living her dreams, she produced a life of success, fame, and fortune even though she experienced a hard childhood. We learned about her life from the movie, *"What's Love Got to Do with It"* and that her marriage to Ike Turner was filled with mental and physical abuse. But Tina Turner's past couldn't stop her. She became a trailblazer.

Paul Prudhomme — The youngest of thirteen children, Chef Paul (Paul Prudhomme), learned the love of cooking at an early age by spending time in the kitchen with his mother. Like Tina Turner and so many others who have earned the title "Successful", Chef Paul's family were share-croppers.

Though raised on a farm he was determined to learn and do what he loved, which was cooking. His determination turned him into a "celebrity chef" ... famous for his Cajun cuisine. From my studies I learned that more successful people, who know how to handle fame and fortune, typically come from a childhood of humble beginnings. Tina Turner, Chef Paul and many others built powerful careers. Without a generous inheritance or even a family structure to fall back on they applied hard work and used the talent they were blessed with to live their dreams.

Bill Clinton — Former President Bill Clinton's biological father died in an automobile accident three months before he was born. His stepfather was an alcoholic and gambler. However, Clinton didn't sit in pity over his dysfunctional stepfather's habits. He made good grades in school; he was an active student leader, an avid reader, and musician. He had a focus for his life at sixteen years old; he knew he wanted to be in public life as an elected official. I, along with many others, consider him as one of our greatest American presidents.

Something bigger. — Stepparents can make or break a child. Later in this book you will read how my father's stepmother could have broken him forever. A person must find in life something "to do" bigger than the abuse they've experienced. That is why successful people (coming from abuse) go so deep inside, and use the abuse as a driving force to achieve their dreams. They are looking for something to break the constant reminder and sting of the abuse. If the energy inside is not utilized in a positive way, the drive or determination (for life) is consumed with the thoughts of what happened. But those thoughts can be replaced with a drive to live with purpose and expect something bigger.

Harry Belafonte — Determination will win out. Harry Belafonte is known as a singer, songwriter and actor. In an interview he shared the difficulties of his childhood before becoming his *authentic* self. When he was a young child his parents divorced and he move from New York to Jamaica to live with relatives. He later moved back to New York. There was a time when his life seemed to have no direction. He said in an interview that he worked odd jobs to survive (one was an assistant to a janitor). He soon found his *authentic* calling after attending a performance at the American Negro Theater. Belafonte had to deal with the success and struggles of Hollywood. It was his determination that won out and earned him the fame of his career; and it was his perseverance for justice that he became a powerful social activist in the pursuit of social justice.

Joyce Meyer — I attended one of Joyce Meyer's earlier ministry-conferences at a hotel (a small room of ladies attending). She spoke about being sexually abused by her father; the poverty and rejection she suffered from others. Through her pain she fought for her *authentic* life. Her triumph prepared her to help others get through their pain. Think about it! The abuse didn't stop her from living her life without purpose. If you are singing, "Woe is me" then you'll get more "Woe is me". You have to get up and take small steps like Joyce Meyer. Her ministry started off small, but it grew into a worldwide ministry, best-selling books and so much more. She experienced pain and abuse (as Andre Crouch sings "Through It All"); but she used it to do more with her life than others who have gone through less.

Matthew Lewis — The word "kind-hearted" describes Matthew Lewis. He is a successful business man (living near my hometown of Woodbury, Georgia). However, before the success came he and his family were the original Ingalls (from the Little House on the Prairie series). He lived in a little house on the hill raising their family and struggling to survive. Then Matthew started a cleaning service. He often had to leave family dinners because one of his employees didn't show up, and it was his responsibility to get the cleaning done (sometimes tired from just finishing up a previous job). He never complained about the lack of good help or mumbled about the lack of money in the business. However, after becoming successful, he told me how the business sometimes didn't make enough money to pay the employees, and his wife would use her paycheck (from teaching school), to help him. But, they never quit. They pulled together and persevered.

Success won. — One day, while looking through a neighborhood newspaper I came across a story on Matthew Lewis. We had not talked in a while but there he was receiving accolades for the success of his business, the contributions he was making in the neighborhood, providing employment, and rebuilding his church for the community. He had turned a struggling little cleaning service into a high tech janitorial and vending machine business. Major contracts had come his way. The little house on the hill was now the mansion on the hill. His wife no longer had to teach school. His family members were appointed to oversee many of the offices he opened in other nearby towns. Moreover, Matthew was invited to the White House (during the term of President Bill Clinton) to sit in on the Board of Small Business Owners. It's amazing how determined success wins in a situation that looks like nothing will happen. The key to Matthew's success was his never wavering (good) attitude through it all. He kept a winning, kind, and friendly spirit all the way to the bank. Matthew and his family are *authentic.*

Percy Jayceon Miller — Many people allow their living conditions to stop them and confine their mind from living a successful life. Percy Jayceon Miller (better known by his stage name Master P) grew up in a rough neighborhood (the projects) in New Orleans; however, the environment didn't stop him from becoming an entertainer and entrepreneur. He is the successful founder and CEO of P. Miller Enterprises and he's responsible for so many other successful endeavors. His perseverance opened the door for his famous son Romeo Miller (previously Lil' Romeo) and I'm sure that many others gained success by stepping through the wide open door Master P made available. Many rappers left the streets (violence and crime), and turned their poverty and pain into a successful lifestyle.

Thomas DeCarlo Callaway — Who knew Thomas DeCarlo Callaway (better known by his stage name Cee-Lo), would become a successful singer, rapper, songwriter and record producer — celebrity? I met him at church and I was also the graphic designer for his mother's bridal-shop. I knew him as Carlo. (Both of us were in his mother's fashion show, but never interacted). He was quiet and didn't show any signs (to me) that he was a powerhouse of talent, but it was there awaiting its opportunity. Carlo once said in an interview that he put all of his focus and energy into his music after the death of his mother; and as we all know, Carlo (Cee-Lo) is a big-name in the music industry. At that time, it didn't look like it, but Carlo was Cee-Lo all along and just awaiting his time to become his *authentic* self.

Shawn Brooks — Shawn is so talented and I personally give him the credit for motivating me and sparking the creativity within me to write my first book. Out of his pain he chose to motivate others. His parents died when he and his siblings were young. Not having the traditional family structure didn't hinder him from pursuing a successful career. "Failure", he said, "was never an option." Out of hard times and trying other professions, he finally found his passion and love for photography. I can personally testify that he makes the camera love on you. He is also an excellent graphic designer and has designed a gorgeous website for me (www.josieslatonterry. com). In his world of photography, publishing his magazines and many other forms of graphic creativity, he found his *authentic* self. *"I capture the moment."* ~Shawn Brooks

Paul Shepherd aka "OCK" — Paul is another Stevie Wonder. He is simply amazing on the harmonica. There was a time when Paul suffered through marital hurt, but he chose to reinvent his life. At the height of everything looking "gloom and doom", Paul taught himself to play the harmonica. Today, OCK performs at the Fabulous over Forty

Networking functions and at other venues. OCK is doing something that came out of his pain–playing his harmonica to inspire others.

Madonna — Authentic people come out on top. In an interview with a major magazine, Madonna said, "As a youth I was a lonely girl who was searching for something. I wasn't rebellious in a certain way. I didn't shave my underarms and I didn't wear make-up like normal girls do. But I studied and I got good grades; I cared about being good at something. I wanted to be somebody." Madonna did just that. Her early life was filled with loss, hurt and pain, but she kept going and came out on top.

Dave Thomas — Authentic people become successful. David "Dave" Thomas, Chief Executive Officer of Wendy's Old Fashioned Hamburgers (a fast-food restaurant), lived a rewarding life. He could have complained and blamed everything on his childhood, but he turned his pain into becoming a successful businessman. He could have wallowed in his sorrows; after all, he was born to a young unwed mother he never knew. He could have blamed her for giving him up for adoption, but as an adult outside of his business success, he became a well-known advocate for adoption; he formed the Dave Thomas Foundation for Adoption in 1992. Although not typical, some adopted individuals want to feel confused and lost (by choice). Even with the best adopted parents…adopted children could still give them "hell". I had a neighbor who adopted a son; he felt like someone had to pay for him not being wanted by his birth mother. What would happen if those individuals would be thankful that someone gave birth to them so they could play a wonderful role in this world? What would happen if they shifted their focus to use their life to bless others instead of dwelling on why they were given up for adoption? The answer could be that they would become another Dave Thomas…becoming successful (their *authentic* self) by using their success to help others.

Cher — Wrong turns in life will not stop a person destined to live their success story. I read when she was a child, Cher was once placed in foster care; she was diagnosed with dyslexia and left high school at the age of 16. With all of that behind her and hanging over her head she could have been discouraged enough to quit. Nevertheless, Cher became a pop singer-songwriter, actress, director and record producer. She has won an Academy Award, a Grammy Award, an Emmy Award, three Golden Globe Awards and a People's Choice Award for her work in film, music and television. There was no way to see this kind of life happening based on a bad start in life, but it's possible.

A constant rebirthing. — Life celebrates people who are doers and not weepers, who languish over their misfortunes. Some people continue to reflect over what happened to them in the first grade and now they are past forty years old. The memories of how something went wrong or how somebody did them wrong are still fresh as if the offense happened yesterday. Always remember that you're not living in regret when life feels richer and is full of meaning. At this point, you're aware that life has more to offer; you live life appreciating every minute of the day and you live in the freedom of thinking and understanding how to be your *authentic* self. Rebirthing new dreams can be through admiring the loveliness of nature, in the melody of a beautiful song, in a striking portrait or in a good play/movie.

Preparation is the key. — It's about living outside of the average realm. You must have expectancy in your heart even when nothing appears to be happening. Alexander Graham Bell said, *"Before anything else, preparation is the key to success."* I am touched by others who have made the necessary changes to live the *authentic* life. They are not sitting back nursing their wounds; instead, they've found the cure by living their purpose:

- Stop procrastination.
- Do what you can and do it well.

- Stop listening to wrong advice.
- Live your dreams and make them a reality.

They became famous. — I always talked about Oprah and how I admire her because she's the epitome of living your *authentic* self. Everyone knows she is a true success story. Before she launched OWN network, I sat down one day and relaxed to watch Oprah's daily talk show (The Oprah Winfrey Show). On this particular day, the topic was about the jobs celebrities held before they became famous:

- Paula Deen the famous (Southern) chef was featured and she said she once worked as a bank teller for 20 years.
- Kirstie Alley best known in her role as Rebecca on the sitcom *Cheers* and in the movie, *Look Who's Talking,* landed her first job as a housekeeper (as a teenager) before becoming famous.
- Drew Carey is known from (to name a few) *The Drew Carey Show, The Price is Right,* and *Whose Line Is It Anyway?* Before reaching stardom he worked as a bank teller and was also a waiter at Denny's.

There are so many stories of people who started out as cooks or dishwashers, but ultimately became owner of the restaurant. Some were janitors, but later became CEOs in the building where they once cleaned. The success of the *authentic* life is sweetened by doing "a job well-done" at every level in life. Teacher and Author, Dr. Wayne Dyer explains in his lectures and books that there are no excuses for not living your best life. In his book *Excuses Begone,* Dr. Dyer writes about reversing self-defeating thoughts and living at the highest levels of success, happiness and health. He is proof that one can have an overcoming life.

An authentic happy life. – Instead of entertaining the recurring testimony of how at the age of six someone mistreated you; fill the hurt with charity work and doing positive things for others. There are people to assist you like Dr. Phil and others, who can get you through the childhood and adulthood abuse. Singer, Aretha Franklin sings *"Don't play that song for me, because it brings back memories"*; so stop singing your sad songs because people get tired of hearing it. Positive people like being around other positive people. Martin Seligman is known as the father of positive psychology. He theorizes that while sixty percent of happiness is determined by our genetics and environment, the remaining forty percent is left up to us.

Eckhart Tolle — In the book *The Power of Now* author, Eckhart Tolle talks about living day to day in the moment (now). Tolle described his early life as unhappy and troubled by depression, anxiety and fear. However, the practice of living in the NOW changed his story and the outcome was spell-bounding. Eckhart Tolle lives his *authentic* life in the NOW and is helping others to do the same.

All ears are open when it comes to hearing about triumphing stories — the more the merrier. That's why I'm writing about them. I'm like a kid in a candy store; captivated by stories of men and women who are making a difference in the world. Through the setbacks and hardships, they didn't quit on their story. You never know whose name you will find in history's biographies...keep living to inspire the world... your name may be next. *"Show me a character whose life arouses my curiosity and my flesh begins crawling with suspense."* ~Fawn M. Brodie

Grow In Pain

Chapter 5:

L ife's pains and trials are just opportunities for new doors to open. Pain will stretch you and educate you, if you allow it to do so. Pain also helps you to find your *authentic* self, if you use it use right. I had a friend who talked about her pain day and night. It was her friend and companion. She did not understand as country singer, Kenny Rogers said (paraphrasing) "You got to know how to fold, hold, and how to walk away" from a thing. My friend did the first two, but not the last. She allowed the pain to wake her up and to take her to bed. That is the outcome of pain controlling and dictating your life with negative words: "You can't continue living, "Forget your dreams", "It's over" and "No one cares about you or your dreams". You can stop listening to pain by meditating on words of faith, hope, and by understanding that there is a plan for your life through the pain. Men and women living their purpose went through the pain and grew their dreams from it. *"The only power that pain has is the power that comes through your words."~ M. Slaton*

Abraham Lincoln – Mr. Lincoln, the sixteenth President of the United States suffered from a form of depression. However, he successfully led the United States through its greatest internal crisis, the American Civil War, preserving the Union and ending slavery. He is also known as one of the most beloved and admired presidents of the United States of America. *"All my life I have tried to pluck a thistle and plant a flower wherever the flower would grow in thought and mind."* ~Abraham Lincoln

Ludwig van Beethoven – Beethoven had an amazing ability to create and play music even though he was completely deaf. If there was one thing affecting him, it was fighting the emotions (he felt inside when he turned around) looking at the audience as they applauded; he could not hear the applauses, but he felt it. However, this disability did not conquer him and he was one of the greatest musicians of all time. *"Music should strike fire from the heart of man, and bring tears from the eyes of woman."* ~Ludwig van Beethoven

Louise L. Hay — The world was blessed with women like Louise Hay. She worked through the pain: a rocky childhood, raped by a neighbor when she was about 5 years old, dropped out of high school and became pregnant and on her sixteenth birthday … gave up her newborn baby girl for adoption. Nevertheless, she found her *authentic* life, became a motivational author and the founder of Hay House (a successful publishing company). Additionally, she started the Hay House Radio, did a movie entitled, *You Can Heal Your Life,* she created the *You Can Do It* conferences, and the list goes on. Ms. Hay didn't give into the pain, and her life which had so many stop signs has inspired so many — including me. *"The thoughts we choose to think are the tools we use to paint the canvas of our lives."* ~Louise L. Hay

Marvin Slaton — His life spoke for him. Marvin Slaton was born to an unwed mother. He was the only child fathered by Erus Slaton, who was already in a long term marriage to his wife Louise when Marvin was conceived. Talking about a scandal it was worse than the TV series' *Scandal* created 2012 by Shonda Rhimes. Louise developed a hard-heart toward her husband and the child (Marvin) conceived by her husband's mistress. To make matters worse the mistress (Marvin's biological mother) died from an illness when he was 7 years old. The only family he could turn to was his biological father. The father wanted his son; therefore he took him to his home. However, his wife Louise was determined to give them pure hell. Even though she was an educator, she refused to give Marvin a proper education. Therefore, he was sent to work in the cotton fields, while his friends attended school. She constantly told him that he was "no good." The bad treatment from his stepmother left Marvin struggling with low self-esteem, a stuttering problem, and not being able to read or write. *"Let your life speak for you."* ~Marvin Slaton

His life prevailed. — Through the hurt and pain Marvin Slaton's life prevailed. At 19, he married Josephine, who was also in her teens; and their union produced five children who love them profoundly. Marvin worked two jobs to care for his family. After he'd work all morning in the cotton field, next he had to walk ten miles to his job at the factory because he didn't have a car. Marvin said he would be so tired and there were times he didn't think he could carry on but the thought of providing for his family is the very thing that kept him going. His strong values of truth, hard-honest work habits and his decent spirit were embedded into the hearts of his children. They all grew up to live successful lives and proudly passed on Marvin's genuine and strong characteristics to their children. *"I couldn't quit, because I had to take care of my family."* ~Marvin Slaton

An authentic hero. — Proudly, I say Marvin Slaton is my dad. Determined to do the right thing, his pain did not stop him from caring for his ailing stepmother, Mrs. Louise (we were not allowed to call her grandmother); who in her eighties had no one to turn to except her stepson (Marvin). My dad remains in my heart as an *authentic* hero; cherished and valued by his family and friends. As the fourth child born to Marvin and Josephine Slaton, I refuse to allow the pain of life to stop me from reaching my goals. It's my honor to live my dreams in triumph to him. My strength comes from the path my dad paved for me and my siblings. From his pain he became the diamond in the rough for his family, the church, the neighborhood and to every life he touched.

Live a life having others asking for more. – When my dad departed this life in 2005, I knew I would cherish his memories forever in my heart. I just couldn't get enough of his presence. Recently, I was at a Temptation and Four Tops' concert and Lawrence Payton, Jr. sung Luther Vandross' *Dance with my Father,* as a triumph to his father, Lawrence Payton, Sr. (one of the original Four Tops). I saw my dad in a vision dancing with me, telling me jokes and being his wonderful self; and as Lawrence Jr. beautifully echoed the words to the song, tears flowed down my face like rain. Wow! It's wonderful how a person can touch your life so deeply. That was my dad! I'm so thankful he didn't quit on life; and that is why I'm here today with dreams in my heart. Even now, when I think of my wonderful dad – in my heart *"I am dancing with my father, again."*

Bless the pain. – The people causing the pain should be "blessed" and not "cursed"; pain has its value, it's a teacher. There's a saying, "There is more growth in the rain than in the sun." You have to work through the pain. There is a story about a family who passed pain on from one generation to the next. No one said, "Stop!" They accepted life as a malfunction. If the wrong package was delivered to your house you wouldn't accept it. Likewise with life, don't continue a life that's unfulfilling and full of pain; but embrace the fulfilling life that is available for you. Even when everyone in your family is satisfied with a "barely getting along" life, you don't have to accept it. Sure, they will talk about you, but be proud of your title: *Black Sheep of the Family.* One day, they will regret not having the life you were blessed to live.

The Krystal Williams Foundation — Survive the pain. The Krystal Williams Foundation was established in the loving memory of Krystal Williams. On April 22, 2005, Krystal Williams was invited by a friend to another friend's house party. Krystal was shot and killed as she stood outside the house party with her friends. A lovely young lady, only 14 years old was shot and killed by a member of a gang (driving by) that she knew nothing about. Krystal was a smart and active student at Forest Park High School in Forest Park, Georgia. At her funeral, you could tell by the attendance that she was loved by so many. I worked closely with the mother and grandparents as they made preparations for the first banquet in her honor. They used their pain to help stop this kind of violence from happening to someone else. They established The Krystal Williams Foundation (KWF) whose mission is to provide quality developmental programs which empower the youth, especially those from disadvantaged circumstances, to realize their full potential as productive citizens. KWF accomplishes this mission by delivering quality programs that meet the changing needs of young people. The core areas of impact are: Health, Education, Employability and Leadership Development. They used their pain to stop pain. Krystal Williams' life still lives on because her family chose to gain from pain and to find their *authentic* selves. *"One change always leaves the way open for the establishment of others."* ~Niccolo Machiavelli

More than Fame

Chapter 6:

P eople living their *authentic* lives are philanthropists. In one of President Barack Obama's quotes he states, *"I think when you spread the wealth around its good for everybody."* The rich and famous, Chairman and CEO of Facebook, Mark Zuckerberg, the phenomenal Oprah Winfrey, billionaire investor Warren Buffett, Bill and Melinda Gates (Co-chair of the Bill and Melinda Gates Foundation) are all huge philanthropists. Ann Romney the wife of Mitt Romney (2012 Republican Party's nominee for president) impressed me with her involvement in a number of children charities. These are names you're familiar with who are changing the world with their *authentic* giving; generally, you expect for them to give to charities, college funds and foundations. But always remember there are people you may never hear about who regularly engages in *authentic* giving, because they are *authentic* philanthropists. Whoever you are and wherever you are in life, you can make a difference in the lives of others.

Grace Groner — This story is about Grace Groner, a frugal woman who died at the age of 100. She was born in Lake County, Illinois and made her home in Chicago. In January 2010, her attorney notified Lake Forest College (in Lake Forest, Illinois) that Ms. Groner (who was known for buying clothes from rummage sales and walking instead of buying a car) left her alma-mater seven million dollars. When the attorney informed the school on the amount of the donation, the president of the college shockingly said, "Oh, my God!"

The silent authentic heroes. — That was Grace Groner's story. There is a similar story about another woman who saved the money she made from doing laundry for other people. She donated it to a college so someone could have the education she was denied...that is *authentic*, because everyone can change a life. It's not about the fame, how much you know or how much you have. It's all about using your life where you are right now for the good. The *authentic* person helps others; it's important to use your abundance to help communities in crises. Sadly, I knew people who departed this life and left money in the bank only for their family to fight over it. The *authentic* people invest in the life of others; and leave blessings which live on through good causes. There are so many untold stories of kind deeds by unknown *authentic* givers.

Ed Sullivan – People living their *authentic* lives are funny. Laughter and a good sense of humor are keys to living a balanced and healthy lifestyle. Ed Sullivan had a healthy sense of humor about himself; he permitted and even encouraged famous impersonators (the good and the bad imitators) to mimic him on his show. The impressionists inflated his rigidity, high shoulders, and nasal tenor phrasing, along with some of his commonly used introductions. A good sense of humor is *authentic*. *"If you do a good job for others, you heal yourself at the same time, because a dose of joy is a spiritual cure. It transcends all barriers."* ~ Ed Sullivan

Bill Cosby — Actor, author, television producer, educator, musician and activist, Bill Cosby who was always humorous described himself as the class clown. While vacationing in Las Vegas in the 70's (there to see Bill Cosby's performance), I met him while he was getting on the elevator, and I was getting off. I said, "You are Bill Cosby?" He replied, "Yes" (humorously and politely back to me). I wanted his autograph right there on the spot but I didn't have anything to write with or write on (I was doing what the average fan would do...panic!). Although I never got his autograph it is worthy to note that his graciousness eased my panic. In Atlanta,

I had a chance to also meet his brother Russell. (He once worked at the same company with my brother). Russell was nice and had a good sense of humor like his brother Bill. In 1997, Bill Cosby's son Ennis was killed while changing a flat tire on the side of an interstate. In 2011, Bill Cosby authored the book, *"I Didn't Ask to Be Born: (But I'm Glad I Was)"*. He is an *authentic* funny and kind man even through his pain. *"You can turn painful situations around through laughter. If you can find humor in anything, even poverty, you can survive it."* ~Bill Cosby

Joan Rivers — Authenticity and laughter work well with success. You don't have to be a celebrity to master a good sense of humor. Learning to laugh and having a wittiness about yourself restores the real you. Funny lady, Joan Rivers' humor pokes fun at others and herself. An *authentic* person can laugh at the challenges and turn them into something funny. *"I blame my mother for my poor sex life. All she told me was the man goes on top and the woman underneath. For three years my husband and I slept in bunk beds."* ~Joan Rivers

Jim Carrey — Comedian Jim Carrey has been described as one of the biggest movie stars in Hollywood and he has received the awards to prove it. Jim's early beginnings did not mirror his current success. His biography says he never finished high school because he worked full-time to help his family survive a severe economic hardship, and he also helped care for his ailing mother. Jim said in an interview, if his career in show business had not worked out, he would probably be working at the steel mill (in the town where he and his family resided). Jim had a dream to live above his circumstances. His dream came true. His high energy and slapstick performances (*authentic* self) entertain the world. *"It is better to risk starving to death than surrender. If you give up on your dreams, what's left?"* ~Jim Carrey

Rodney Dangerfield — "Take my family...please." Something that funnyman Rodney Dangerfield would say. He had a rough start. His father abandoned the family. He was fired from his job as a singing waiter; as he would later coin it "No Respect." His big break came through The Ed Sullivan Show when Ed Sullivan needed a last minute replacement, and the rest is history. He found his *authentic* self and respect through laughter. *"What a kid I got, I told him about the birds and the bees and he told me about the butcher and my wife."* ~Rodney Dangerfield

An authentic family. — People living their *authentic* lives share family values. My family was funny. "Not funny-farm funny" though, that shouldn't be ruled out. Nevertheless, when we are together we make each LOL (laugh out loud). It started with my dad, then my mother, passed down to my brothers Melvin, Calvin, Aaron, to my sister Jean and myself, and then to our extended family members. Laughter was (and is) our strength… making each other laugh over any and everything. We believe "a family that laughs together stays together". My mother, who was the main comedian in our family, beat breast cancer because of her sense of humor and laughter (together with her faith). She was the original Lucille Ball. *"After God created the world, He made man and woman. Then, to keep the whole thing from collapsing, He invented humor." ~Bill Kelly "Mordillo"*

Erykah Davenport. — My great-niece, Erykah Davenport was possibly the tallest girl in her class. I'm sure she wondered, "Why do I have to be so tall?" People always make comments when you are very tall, short, fat, skinny, dark, light or whatever. You can't please everyone, and in addition to that, you didn't make yourself. So, what do you do? My advice is to develop a "nevertheless" attitude. Nevertheless, Erykah grew up to be a beautiful, elegantly-tall and smart young lady. What happened to Erykah? (It's a lesson for us all). She used her height to become a superstar-basketball player. The likelihood of this happening was not in Erykah's corner. She didn't grow up with a father in the home; she didn't come from a wealthy family, and her mother worked around-the-clock to support Erykah and her brother Erus.

Quovadis, my niece and Erykah's mother (a wise mother) sent Erykah to summer camp during the summer to keep her busy. God bless wonderful mentors; the wonderful summer camp coaches took notice of Erykah and groomed her for the game. The years of playing basketball prepared her once she became a senior in high school, to be selected as one of Georgia's 2014 top girls-basketball recruits. As she approaches graduation (from Tucker High School) Erykah 6'3" is receiving a full scholarship to a major college. The very tall girl ... did it! Through dedication to the game she fought for the right to start a super *authentic* life.

Refuse to give-up. — People living their *authentic* lives are on a journey (not just for the fame) to live out what they are called to do. The dream keeps them alive. I know people who were diagnosed with serious illnesses, but are living a healthy and successful lifestyle today...the dream kept them alive. They live with purpose and refuse to give-up. They know their best days are still ahead. When you have a dream to live it's never the end, but a new beginning ... if you don't give-up. *"An individual's self-concept is the core of his personality. It affects every aspect of human behavior: the ability to learn, the capacity to grow and change. A strong, positive self-image is the best possible preparation for success in life."* ~Dr. Joyce Brothers

Just Be You

Chapter 7:

The successful *authentic* YOU knows that true happiness is found in the soul and not in material things. You know every opportunity opens in its own time and the *authentic* you wait willingly while filling your life with devoted activities, and the spirit of love as your medicine of choice. Success does not change you from being a good person. Success and prosperity make you more of YOU. Someone once commented on meeting Celine Dion said, "I could feel the love radiating from her, it was as beautiful as her singing." Celine Dion once said in an interview that she remains grounded by doing good deeds and spending time with her family. *"But the fruit of the Spirit is love, joy, peace, longsuffering, gentleness, goodness, faith, meekness and temperance..."* ~ (Galatians 5:22-23, KJV)

Dr. Elon Bomani — Do not be ashamed of YOUR life... use it to help others. I saw a wonderful lady, Dr. Elon Bomani who played in the Hayhouse movie, *You Can Heal Your Life* by Louise Hay. She did a short cameo, but her words stood out and triggered in me to learn more about her life. I read that she went from being a homeless mother with $36 dollars in her checking account to millionaire status in 18 months by investing in real-estate, trading, network marketing and internet marketing. Dr. Bomani says her change started when she changed her thoughts. She authored the following top-selling books, *"Dynamic Diva Dollars"*, *"Wealth Chants"* and *"Good Debt Riches"*; Dr. Bomani said, *"I changed my thoughts, my words and my actions for the better. I was good at creating my hell. Now, I am in the business of creating my heaven. I fell madly in love with myself and live my best life now. What a difference, a thought can make."*

Be the best YOU. — There are many people who are living their purpose and being their *authentic* self; helping others like Dr. Elon Bomani, but you may never hear about them. They are the parents, teachers and community leaders imparting wisdom to the next generation. They care enough to reach out and help young people to have a valuable life. Dr. Elon Bomani also said, *"If you want to be a millionaire, you have got to hang out with millionaires and do some of the things that millionaires do."*

- Talk to yourself in the mirror, "Today, I will be my most excellent self."

- Love the skin you are in.
- Don't be afraid to try something new.
- Surround yourself with good friends.
- Helping others will help you to be your best self.
- Learn to laugh and have fun.

Les Brown — "It's possible to live YOUR dream!" Les Brown (Motivational Speaker, Speech Coach, and Best-Selling Author) was speaking in downtown Atlanta, Georgia during the late 90's. There was heavy traffic on the road. I cannot remember if it was cold or rainy (all I remember is that I had a one track mind) as my friends and I traveled to hear Les Brown speak but it was worth whatever we had to go through to get there. We left the lecture highly impacted with the motivation we needed. In his biography it says before Les Brown pursued a career as a motivational speaker, he was broke and slept on the cold linoleum floor of his office. Of course, if you have ever heard Mr. Brown speak, you know his early beginning did not predict the kind of success he achieved in life. Born on the floor of an abandoned building, he and his twin brother were adopted by Ms. Mamie Brown, a 38-year-old unmarried cafeteria cook and domestic worker. "The importance of her entrance into his life," Brown concludes, "was immeasurable." His famous quote, *"Everything I am and everything I have I owe to my mother."* While speaking at a renowned church, Les Brown shared some of his health issues, and other things he had gone through. As he spoke I saw how his trials made him even more polished. Twenty years later (from the first time I traveled with my friends through rush hour traffic to hear Les Brown speak), I still conclude that he's the master *authentic* motivator for the soul. *"It takes someone with a vision of the possibilities to attain new levels of experience. Someone with the courage to live his dreams."* ~Les Brown

YOU need a positive mindset. – While shopping at the vitamin shop a charming man stood behind the counter. He was there with so many wonderful vitamins, in which some of them he consumed faithfully. His negative mindset was the only thing I observed as he talked. I thought to myself, "He's pouring all of those good vitamins into a body full of negative energy." He began saying to me, "My body is falling apart because of age. I will never have the good health I once had." He tried to get me to agree with him as he said all of these negative things about himself. He kept on, "You are going to have aches and pain. Old age will work against you." Finally, he stopped talking and I thought, "Wow! It was good that I came in with a strong and positive mindset." Beware of negative conversations. When people have a negative outlook, they can have billions of dollars in the bank, but still think they are broke. Just like positive people are contagious, negative people are infectious. Colin Powell, the 65th United States Secretary of State said, *"Surround yourself with people who take their work seriously, but not themselves; those who work hard and play hard."*

Being YOU is not about being perfect. – Taking everything into consideration and doing your best; it's hard trying to think you can be perfect. If you give life the best you have and live the dream in your heart then you've earned the merit "job well done." The moment you were born, Touchdown! Your journey - to become who you were meant to be - was activated. You should not take your birth as a mishap. You are meant to be here. You have a reason for being here. Your purpose is bigger than "how you got here." Everything becomes clearer once you stop playing the blame game, let go of the hurt, and discover your purpose. As with my dad who I wrote about in chapter five; he was hurt by cruel acts of his stepmother, but he came out on top through forgiveness and he found purpose in caring for her (in her time of need) and his entire family.

Mo'Nique — Living who YOU were meant to be means … growing beyond the shame. The biography of comedian, actress and talk show host Mo'Nique says that during an interview with Essence magazine, Monique disclosed that she was sexually abused by her brother from the age of seven until eleven years old. However, she faced the shame and hurt. She didn't allow her past to stop her. Mo'Nique is honored and loved for her work. (I still love to watch the reruns of her TV show, "The Parkers"). She moved on to enjoy a successful life. When shame and hurt doesn't stop you from being who you are...that's *authentic!*

Your forgiveness is authentic. — The power of being your *authentic* self is in forgiveness; forgiving yourself and the other person. During an interview Oprah asked author and poet, Dr. Maya Angelou (who was raped as a child), "What advice would you give to yourself looking back?" Dr. Angelou replied, "To forgive." Because of forgiveness she has known success in such powerful measures; even speaking before presidents and other great leaders. *"Bitterness is like cancer..."* ~Dr. Maya Angelou

Susan Boyle — When others put you down don't worry, YOU will have the last laugh, if you stick with your life's plan. Susan Boyle had the last laugh. The Scottish singer came into the public eye internationally when she appeared as a contestant on a reality TV show (Britain's Got Talent, April 2009) singing, *I Dreamed a Dream*. She came on the stage with a plain unappealing appearance; but her powerful voice overwhelmed everyone that was under the sound of it. Her first album was released in November 2009 and debuted as the number one best-selling CD. Susan came through a difficult birth and was later diagnosed as having learning difficulties. As a child she said she was bullied. After leaving school (with few qualifications) it was stated she was employed for the only time in her life as a trainee cook in the kitchen of a college for six months. Her seed was her voice and she performed at a number of local venues. Susan Boyle, the girl nicknamed "Susie Simple" at school … had the last laugh.

Jim Nabors — YOU fit the profile for your purpose. Long before there was a Susan Boyle there was actor and singer, Jim Nabors with his lovable personality. Born and raised in Alabama, his biography says he moved to California due to his asthma. While working at a Santa Monica nightclub, he was discovered by Andy Griffith and consequently joined The Andy Griffith Show, playing Gomer Pyle, a dim-witted gas station attendant. The character proved popular, and Nabors was given his own spin-off show, Gomer Pyle, U.S.M.C. He didn't look the part, but he had a golden voice. His voice didn't fit his looks, but that's how life is. You don't fit the profile the world thinks you should fit; but you succeed anyway. *"Aerodynamically, the bumble bee shouldn't be able to fly, but the bumble bee doesn't know it so it goes on flying anyway."* ~Mary Kay Ash

Jaleel White — If YOU are nerdy...two thumbs-up. There was a time when people laughed at nerds. Jaleel White's character was the lovable and nerdy Urkle, who became admired by fans for his role in the sitcom, "Family Matters". In today's time being a nerd (overly intellectual and a socially-square) is a good thing. They are usually the ones designing software and becoming billionaires. You don't have to be a beauty queen or body builder to have *authentic* success. Life is full of triumphs for everyone who works with what they have and live their *authentic* dream.

Dolly Parton — If YOU grew up poor, you are in good company. Best known for her work in country music, Dolly Parton is a successful singer, songwriter, actress, author and businesswoman. Born in Tennessee she was described as being "dirt poor". Dolly Parton is a cultural icon whose shapely figure and powerful voice (though at first criticized) has made her a leader in her profession. *"I'm not offended by dumb blonde jokes because I know that I'm not dumb; I also know I'm not blonde."* ~Dolly Parton

Alice Walker — YOU have greatness in you. The parents of author, Alice Walker supported her in having an education. It was during a time when black sharecroppers' children were supposed to stay home from school and work in the field with their parents. When she was around eight years old, Alice's brother shot her in the eye with a BB gun. Behind that incident, Alice became blind in one eye. She became self-conscious and shy. She spent more time reading and writing poetry. Alice Walker grew from her afflictions, becoming the valedictorian and queen of her senior class. After high school she attended Spelman College in Atlanta, Georgia. In 1982, she published what has become her best known work, *"The Color Purple"*.

Whoopi — If YOU feel your success will never happen, think again. Whoopi Goldberg's film debut was *The Color Purple*. Did Whoopi (known to the world as a comedienne, actress and talk show host) know she had so much to offer life while working in the mortuary? In the movie *The Color Purple,* Mister Albert Johnson's (played by Danny Glover) girlfriend name Shug (played by Margaret Avery) told Celie (Whoopi Goldberg), "You sure is ugly." Celie Harris Johnson, a poor, severely abused young black girl, is the underdog. But she didn't lose her dream to reconnect with her real family. The woman, who called her ugly, became the friend who helped her make the reconnection with her family possible. To every person that has experienced rejection, abuse or you just don't fit the status quo, your day is coming! Your color of success is *authentic.* Proverbs 16:7 says, *"When a man's ways please the Lord, he maketh even his enemies to be at peace with him."*

Never Stop Dreaming

Chapter 8:

W alt Disney is known to the world as an animator, filmmaker, and entrepreneur. He dreamed so big that his dream earned him over twenty-two *Academy Awards*. He also founded both *Disneyland* in California and *Walt Disney World* in Florida. Walt Disney said, *"All our dreams can come true - if we have the courage to pursue them."* What about your dreams? Have you ever had those moments when you asked yourself, "Where am I going with my life?" You were supposed to be a great singer, actor, musician, writer, or some other profession, but you found yourself lost in a field of work that doesn't allow you to have any personal time. You have a burning desire to fulfill your dream, but you don't know where to start. Like others who have traveled this road, you have to be creative and make it work anyway. You have to use your time wisely, work out a strategy, and put effort into what means the most to you. Don't stop believing in your dreams; they will come true. Also, consider allowing time and faith to work for you. The bible says, "God will not withhold any good thing from you." Therefore, if you stop being concerned with the how(s) and when(s), the dream will manifest when it's time.

Stay on course. — I met a lady who sings; she told me how her first husband abused her and she lost her love to sing. However, the marriage ended and she eventually met the right person for her life. She started singing and performing again. The gift to sing was never lost in her, but being in an abusive marriage got her off course. Myles Munroe said, *'The poorest man in the world is the man without a dream. The most frustrated man in the world is a man with a dream that never becomes a reality."*

How to stay on course:

- Stay determined to live your dreams.
- Never lose focus of your dreams.
- Get organized in your planning space.
- Visit online sites that help support your dreams.
- Make changes if needed, but stay focused and on course.

Keep moving. — Don't let your dreams die. The mountains you are facing will move! When everyone, every place, and of course when you are ready, the dream will happen. Destiny will meet you at the place you should be, so don't keep moving around from place to place, and from job to job. Follow your heart and know the place where you should be; don't allow others to move you off of your course. When you understand that your dream will happen at the set time then you will be content while you wait. So stay where you are and be at peace. Know you can take whatever is thrown at you, because you are going to the "next level." The next level is living your dreams and becoming your *authentic* self. Do not allow anyone to talk you out of your dreams. Theodor Seuss Geisel, better known as Dr. Seuss (publishing over 60 children's book) said, *"Be who you are and say what you feel, because those who mind don't matter and those who matter don't mind."*

Face your giants. – As of right now, you could be a struggling playwright, but in the next moment you could become a Tyler Perry or John Singleton. Your gift is your seed to greatness. Every new day gives you a chance to move closer to your dream or enter into your dream. Watch for the signs like a door closing, a job ending; the relationship is over, or your body is experiencing pain. These things are the giants of life trying to get your attention; so when you recognize this, don't allow them to rob you of your vision. As you listen to your spirit, you will know the dream is not over; but the page is turning to a new chapter in your life.

Tyler Perry — The problems do not dictate the future. In one interview, actor and director Tyler Perry said he had to sleep in his car because he used his rent money to financially support his play. Personal sacrifices have to be considered when you want the doors of success to open. There is no easy way around it. We learn from Tyler Perry that we cannot give up on our dreams. He believed there was more and he stayed with it. His first stage play, "I know I've Been Changed", was débuted around 1990. He didn't quit because of the negative reviews he received; he simply rewrote the play. Success came for him through his stage plays, films and television productions. Tyler Perry is proof that you should stay true to your *authentic* dream. You may be in the dress rehearsal stage of your life, but success is on the way!

John Singleton — Filmmaker, John Singleton knows even with success you will still face hard challenges. In 2007, he was involved in a car accident in L.A. The filmmaker accidentally struck a woman with his SUV, who was jaywalking; though it was fatal for her, Singleton was proven not guilty of any crime. It was treated as an unfortunate accident and no criminal charges were filed against him. It's still a hardship and you have to find the strength to continue when things go wrong along the way. Nevertheless, don't ever quit your purpose in life.

Rebecca Gayheart — In 2001, actress Rebecca Gayheart also experienced a life challenging ordeal. While driving her vehicle she struck a nine-year old boy as he walked across the street (he died from his injuries). In an interview she said, "It's something that is with me every day, and it will be for the rest of my life." Life has so many unknown challenges. But the mission of the journey is not over because the problem knocked you down, and with every trial there is an end. You must first learn to forgive yourself. There will be unexpected mistakes and life's tests happening on the journey. However the purpose of your life must still be lived, and there are solutions to every painful trial: forgiveness and love. Businessman and writer Paul Boese wrote, *"Forgiveness does not change the past, but it does enlarge the future."*

It's not over.– I mentioned to someone that I was never a great cook; however, taking cooking lessons is one of my goals in life. The person I told this to said, "It's too late; you should have learned how to cook when you were younger." In spite of this, I looked at my belief system and said, "As long as I am breathing, it is never too late to learn new things." God will redeem the time for you when you believe. It's only too late if you think it's too late. Everything that belongs to you is in your words. Do not allow others to speak against your future. You may have people wearing you out with "it's too late" stories, but you must know your truth. As long as you are on the planet earth, it is never too late. True, some things are no longer your desire, but never suspend matters of the heart. Life is like a candle, it will keep burning, until it is used up. Keep learning, growing, loving, laughing and living on the journey with a "wow" and admiration of God's awesomeness.

Betty White – Her smile says it all. I watched Betty White on "The Mary Tyler Moore Show", "The Golden Girls", "Hot in Cleveland" and the reruns of the "Match Game." Always the same beautiful smile. If she had woes and cares, she didn't show it. In her 80's her career grew stronger; she even became a "sex symbol." During this time it was announced that she was posing for her own calendar, featuring photos from her career, and pictures of various animals for which she loved so much. Betty White is still irresistible to her fans as she celebrated her 90th birthday on January 17, 2013. If you once had negative thoughts about your age and the outcome of life, you need to start over with a fresh thought pattern. Life will be what you believe it to be. Positive thoughts will manifest and negative thoughts will do the same. Each day you produce what you think and speak. *"Thoughts become things...choose the good ones!"* ~Mike Dooley

Watch your confessions. – People will try to convince you to confess with them how bad things are. "You see the economy is getting worse and worse." When you try to speak positive about the economy, they'll start telling you what the news report says. It becomes a big drawn out conversation. Guard your ears and your heart. Some people stump their toe and it becomes a serious health issue; while others fall from a tree and survive. To live the *authentic* life you cannot listen to others speaking unconstructively about your future. If they want to be snared by their confessions don't follow suit, fill your heart with words of faith. Be determined to live your life confessing what you want to happen with the expectation that you and God will make it a reality.

Keep the faith. — What do you want from life? Eleanor Roosevelt said, *"The future belongs to those who believe in the beauty of their dreams."* To keep your dreams beautiful, you must water your thoughts like you water plants with necessary nourishment:

- Positive words keep the mind renewed.
- A vision-board will help you to stay on track.

- Staying away from worrywarts will keep you strong.
- Do not allow others to draw the goal line for your future.

The multitude believes "prayer changes things" but some things are not changed immediately. Persistent faith in the dream must be applied until the prayer is answered. You cannot have the clear mind needed to live a wonderful life with negative words from others playing in your mind. You need positive energy to achieve your goals in life. God gave you one life to live and as stated in the poem by Matthew Bill, "You are the Captain of Your Ship." *"We need to find the courage to say no to the things and people that are not serving us if we want to rediscover ourselves and live our lives with authenticity."* —Barbara DeAngelis

Goodness is coming. — You can't pretend to be someone else and live your dream. It would be like the lady who had a facelift to impress the man she wanted to marry, but he refused to marry her because he could not bring himself to marry a woman he didn't recognize. You've got to be you! Trying to be someone else is a waste of valuable time. If someone doesn't want you to be who you really are, the problem is with the other person and not you. Never give anyone the power to stop you from living your dreams. A person cannot defeat you by their judgments and tabloid news, so don't be vexed. Your day of goodness is coming. You will be a winner if you don't get frustrated and give up. Life is not set up for honest, hard work and good deeds to go unrewarded.

Forgiveness and Love

Chapter 9:

Forgiveness and love are doors in your *authentic* walk of life. Peter asked Jesus, "How many times to forgive a person…seven times seven?" Jesus said, "Seventy times seven." Seven is considered as the number of perfection. But it wasn't enough. Seventy-times seven is the number of eternity; meaning you shouldn't keep a record of the offense. Once the offense has been worked out with the other person—you must find a way to move on. If you cannot love them face to face, then love them from afar. Holding onto un-forgiveness will hurt you more than the other person. It will drain the positive energy out of your life and hinder the planning of your life's advancement. You have to accept the forgiveness for yourself and give forgiveness to others.

Maria Cole — She made the main thing "the main thing". During the Christmas holiday, my dad would always sing "Chestnut Roasting over an Open Fire." He loved the way Nat King Cole song the "Christmas Song." He was definitely my father's favorite singer. While reading Nat King Cole's biography, I became impressed with Maria Hawkins Ellington (Maria Cole), his second wife. Nat King Cole died when he was only forty-five and Maria Cole died forty-four years later. It is written that Nat King Cole had a number of affairs during his marriage to Maria, yet she remained focused on her husband's legacy instead of lingering in resentment over his infidelity. She kept his faithful fans thinking about his life's achievements and the spectacular songs he made. If you didn't read about it, you definitely didn't know about the affairs. Surely, she loved her husband, and it would not be too much to assume (as with any spouse in her situation) that extra marital affairs hurt. Nevertheless, Maria Cole was a woman of integrity and she understood the deeper meaning of Nat King Cole's gift to the world. Maria Cole is an unsung *authentic* wife and the mother of one of my favorite singers, Natalie Cole.

Forgiveness does not make you less. — Like Maria Cole, many wives have forgiven their husbands and likewise, many husbands have forgiven their wives of affairs for the betterment of the family, and the dreams they are birthing. No one is in denial of an affair, but when you get to the root you realize the problem (in many cases) can be resolved with love and forgiveness. Forgiveness does not make you less of a person; instead, it makes you more of your *authentic* self. Love is not weakness; love is a strength that helps you to survive the most difficult crisis. If you are to be the person you are destined to be, the outcome where you're going is going to be based on the problems you resolve along the way. The commandment on your *authentic* journey is: "Thy must forgive and love the people who hurt you."

Forgiveness and self-acceptance. – There was a time when I looked in the mirror to tell myself, "I love you" as Louise Hay said to do. But before the words could come out, I started fault-finding. However, through confessions of God's love I finally found the confidence to say to myself, "I love you". During conversation with a friend, they shared their thoughts about how one of our acquaintances was ugly; I wondered how someone can look physically beautiful to one person, and not beautiful to another. After all, beauty is in the eye of the beholder. I have also heard that true beauty is the way a person feels confident about who they are; this allows their authentic self to stand out. When a person cannot see the beauty in you, see the beauty in yourself and live life to be your most awesome self. A comedian once said in an interview, "People didn't think I was handsome until I became famous." He said laughingly, "I am the same person now that I was back then." Success speaks!

Be and love yourself. — One day while in a hair salon getting my hair done, a short average-looking man walked in with a tall beautiful-stallion of a woman. Through my eyes they didn't match as a couple at all. As he walked past the gazing stylists, it was like a Rock Star had entered the salon. They all stopped to greet him. I asked my stylist, "Who is he?" and she said, "Honey, he is a successful man." Another stylist jumped in the conversation adding, "Girl, he manufactures all of the hair products we use in this salon." Both stylists continued with great enthusiasm and raved over the success of this average-looking man. So, I took a second look at him and in my eyes he had gotten taller. The more I heard about him, the more he began to look like a "Hollywood movie star." Now I could see what his beautiful companion saw – a powerful man working his *authentic* life. He spent twenty minutes in the salon greeting and chatting with everyone. When he left the salon his magic continued to engulf the room and everyone felt it. My dad would always say, "It's not what others thinks about you; but what are you thinking about yourself?"

Andraé Crouch — Gospel singer, pastor and songwriter Andraé Crouch had a stuttering problem until he was fourteen so he decided to let his sister, Sandra talk for him in public. The shortcomings will no longer define a person once they enter into their *authentic* self. In the beginning of Andraé Crouch's life he didn't want to talk because he stuttered, but soon found his voice to sing and preach. In my studies I discovered that many famous people had to overcome speaking problems:

- Actress, Julia Roberts admitted that she stuttered when she was younger. But she became an Academy Award-winning actress.
- Singer, Bill Withers best-known for singing *Ain't No Sunshine, Lovely Day* and *Lean on Me.* While in the Navy he underwent speech therapy to overcome a stuttering problem.
- Actor, Samuel L. Jackson was afflicted with a debilitating stuttering problem. He took up acting at the urging of his speech therapist.

"Be yourself. Above all. let who you are, what you are, what you believe shine through every sentence you write, every piece you finish." ~John Jakes

Finding Your Purpose

Chapter 10:

K eep working towards your goal. Actress and comedian Kim Coles best known for her role as Synclaire James on the television show, *Living Single* stated during a discussion on *Exhale* (cable talk show) that, *"You should only be doing what you came here to do."* This is when life makes common sense. Life is about living your heart's desire and fulfilling your dreams at their appointed time. As I ponder over the things in my life "happening" and "not happening", I move with confidence to the next project, because from past experiences I know situations will resolve themselves at the set time. Everything is about understanding your season. Where you are going is bigger than where you are. You have a breakthrough coming, but the closer you get to it the more you want to scream, "Help!" The answer is to start preparing and working toward your goals. You may be at a holding station right now, but soon it will be your time to flap your wings and soar. Bishop Dale Bronner said, *"Your dreams may be delayed, but they will not be denied."*

You have a purpose. – You may be at an age where you're saying, *"Enough is enough!"* You're tired of going to an unfulfilling job and not having the right person in your life. But what do you do? The answer is to fall in love with your purpose (your *authentic* calling). Your purpose will help you to find fulfillment in the midst of the storm. Give time and love to your purpose and you will find yourself transforming into the *authentic* you.

Antwone Fisher — Find yourself. Have you ever seen the movie Antwone Fisher? Based on the book "Finding Fish" which is a 2001 autobiography book by Antwone Fisher, he grew up in the foster care system. His early years in life were scarred by abuse and mistreatment. The inspiring movie is based on the life of Antwone Fisher and directed by one of my favorite actors, Denzel Washington, who played the psychiatrist. It's about an American sailor who connects with the family he longed to know. I learned from watching this story that a sad and painful beginning doesn't have to be your ending.

God will add. — My childhood was not abusive. My father and mother were in the home and they gave my siblings and me as much love as they could possibly give.

I grew up going to church every Sunday morning; I was active in school and in the community. Yet, the day came when I wasn't in search of my family, but I was in search of my *authentic* self. On the journey, I started to realize the heartbreaks and disappointments that I once thought would kill me essentially made me. This is when I buckled down and observed that even the worst part of life held answers to my *authentic* self.

Names have meaning. — There was a time when I believed hurtful words and allowed them to dictate how I felt about myself. For instance, there was a guy I really liked when I was thirteen years old; he didn't like me because he said my name "Josie" was old and ugly. It crushed me. From that time until adulthood, I didn't like my name. That was until I took the time to understand why my mother named me "Josie" — meaning "God will add" and "God is gracious." I also read that people with the name "Josie" have a deep desire for love and companionship, as well as working with others in achieving their harmony and peace. That's me! What a powerful name! It's important for you to take time to learn about yourself and see your uniqueness even when others cannot see it. Luckily, my true friends see me as my name has declared me to be.

On this journey... — There was a time when my husband and I went deep sea fishing. We boarded the boat and were on our way to catch the big one! A snobbish woman and her husband were on board with us. She didn't want to have anything to do with us. She wouldn't speak, smile or sit near us (she was stuck-up). I decided to avoid her as well, because I had no need of her bad personality. Right away the water got choppy around the boat; I was the first to go down...sea sick and sick of the sea! I threw my fishing-rod down. Like an ailing drunk person, my upset stomach was not able to keep anything down. I found a bench and just laid there mourning. With my eyes closed I reached for the person whose head was now touching my head. I thought it was my husband. To my shock, I realized that was not my husband's head! With all the strength I could revive, I looked up. "Oh no; It's that snobbish lady!" I cried inside. I was too sick to move and so was she. The boat was at sea for four hours, but it felt like four years. That lady and I became companions through our sea sickness. She needed me and I needed her for comfort. We made it through the trip together. Once the boat docked, we hugged and waved goodbye. On life's journey you never know who will help get you to the next level. I needed this understanding for my *authentic* journey.

Lost Identity. — I have learned that nothing stays the same. Friends die, couples you never expect get divorced and life happens. It's crazy, but I found pieces of Josie in the things I lost, wrong turns, rejections and heartaches. Just like Antwone Fisher, there is a time you have to go back to where the pain started and get healed to ultimately move on with life. Chapter 9 speaks of *Forgiveness and Love;* once you go back you must forgive and love the guilty party. It's true "hurt people— hurt people." When you lost your identity it was only because you didn't know your value and purpose for life. As you matured into the truth of your life's plan, the new identity had to leave past hurts behind. The baggage of hurtful words, attitudes and rejections are too much to carry and have no place in your *authentic* life.

Finding yourself never stops. — Always remember...you are on a mission. Your journey of finding YOU never stops. Die daily to who you were and live daily to who you are. Refuse to walk around with wrong thoughts such as: "Who did you wrong", or "Who doesn't love you". It's a wonderful discovery to know that your thinking can create a new world that aligns you with the awesomeness of God's mercy and favor. Your mission is to find your *authentic* self and help others to do the same. Think clearly about your life:

-Write down the plans of finding your life's purpose.

-Take responsibility for the things you need to change.

-Trust in yourself more.

David Fonoti — As I develop through life to become more of my *authentic* self, I've always wanted to use my life to help others. Case and point: My oldest brother Melvin is in his sixties and he had an almost similar Antwone Fisher's story in the shadow of his life. The table was turned with him wanting to find a son he had fathered when he was in his twenties. It was around 1969; my brother Melvin was in the Air Force and stationed in Hawaii when he met and started a relationship with a young native girl. She became pregnant and to make a long story short, because of other situations the relationship ended. Melvin had a chance to see his son David come into this world, but that was it. Upon returning home to the mainland all he had in remembrance of his son was a baby picture (his twin). The distance created a loss of connection. In spite of all of the changes, Melvin always mentioned David to his good friend Al Pittman, who remained in Hawaii after completing college. Eventually, through the years my brother lost contact with Al who was his only connection to keep up with how David was doing. There was always a longing in my brother's heart to connect and see David who would now be almost thirty years old. One day my husband and I decided to take a trip to Hawaii for our vacation. After we got settled in our hotel I immediately started searching the hotel's phone directory to find Al Pittman. It was a miracle — I located him! When I told Al that I was Melvin's sister he was so elated that he suggested meeting right away. Al and I met the next day and he gave me all the information I needed to know to locate my brother's son, and my nephew David. He was not in Hawaii; he was in a prison in Texas. This is when I realized that I was not in Hawaii for a vacation, but on a mission to find David. He needed to know there was a family (his family) who wanted to meet and extend their love to him. Speaking of all things working together, my brother's youngest daughter and my niece Angel was station in the Air Force in Texas.

Melvin Slaton — My brother Melvin called his daughter and she immediately went to see David in prison (the older brother she was meeting for the first time). Angel informed him their father wanted to see him, now the ball started rolling. My brother caught the first flight to Texas. He said when he saw David their love for each other was heartfelt. David's first words to him were, "Can I call you dad?" It was definitely a meeting for the good. Upon Melvin's return to the mainland he told us the heart wrenching story of how he pleaded for compassion with the authorities' in-charge (on his son's behalf). He felt his son didn't have the chance to get it right because pieces of his life were missing. He told us about the tears of joy, pain and healing he cried with his son, David. Melvin and David's story became a Lifetime movie...David's father came looking for him to establish a long overdue relationship; and the father welcomed the son home. Melvin welcomed David not only into his life, but into the life of our family. His words to David were, "Now that I've found you, I will never let you go!"

Connected love creates healing. — David's story is healing for anyone seeking a connection within their family. The moral of this story is, if it's within your power; don't leave another person's life unfinished. It's not impossible or too late to change the course of time. Melvin and David connected and stayed connected. But the story gets even better. The time finally came when David returned to Hawaii and his father arranged for him to visit Georgia to meet all of his long awaiting family. The family was there just like in the Antwone Fisher's story. Our love for David was poured on him in large measures from: grandmother, stepmother, sisters, brothers, uncles, aunts and cousins. He was more than what the family could have ever asked for: forgiving, loving, kind and really handsome. It was now real; the David we had heard about was now touchable. This meeting created a beautiful and everlasting union; with the help of modern day social networking everyone stays in touch. During one of our phone calls David said (in his Hawaiian accent), "I love my Georgia family." Of course! I felt the same and (in my Southern) accent I said, "I love my Hawaiian nephew."

Stay Focus

Chapter 11:

S taying focused will turn your doubts into confidence. I was in conversation with a friend who entered into his second marriage. Not operating in good self-confidence he chose a second wife with similar abusive behaviors to the first wife (they both belittled him). Essentially, he was dealing with low self-esteem issues from his childhood and he was working on a job he hated. He looked so dismayed and hopeless. I asked, "What do you want?" He replied, "I don't know." When you don't focus on life an erroneous situations feel normal. Eventually, he started working on his life and putting forth the endeavors to live his *authentic* dreams.

The critics will talk. — Let people have their opinion that's just what it is —an opinion. An opinion is a belief that rests on insufficient judgment. Maybe when you were a child others called you awful names and labeled you as a "nobody", but it doesn't mean you have to live up to that opinion now. You're all grown-up and you know better. The opinion you have about yourself is the only opinion that matters. This is the reason you need to focus on being your *authentic* self. *"One of the recognizable features of the authentic masterpiece is its capacity to renew itself, to endure the loss of some kinds of immediate relevance while still answering the most important questions men can ask, including new ones they are just learning how to frame."* ~Arnold Stein

Focus on the dream — During my twenties, I worked on a job with some ladies that loved to criticize the way I dressed. I was not into their shopping craze (at that time). The latest fashion was a big thing to them. However, my money was used to invest in my education and home. As I moved from that job a few years later, I begin to work on the job of my choice. To my amazement one of the ladies that used to criticize me (at the old job) approached me while I was on a freelancing assignment in downtown Atlanta. She remembered me and called me by name; but I couldn't remember her name. She briefly shared her setbacks with me; she was unemployed and trying to put together the pieces of her life. She left me with some profound words that I keep close to me even today. She said, "I knew you were going to make it, because you were different!" She concluded with, "You never let us distract you or get next to you." That was so insightful to me. Even though I spent many times in the restroom crying from the hurtful comments, she was right; I never lost the determination or focus on my goals because they were and still are so real to me.

The path of the dream. — Stay focused on the road of life. Lighten the load and get off the path of the "He said", "She said" drama. If you feel afraid on the journey of your dreams then feed your faith and starve your doubts. The people who are living their purpose went through the storm. They are not superhuman; they just believed their dreams were possible:

- Remember what you dreamed about when you were a child and write it down.
- Share your dreams with people you trust for more insight.
- Allow the biographies of others to show you how they approached their dreams.

Deborah King — Author Deborah King has a program on Hay House Radio, and on her worldwide program "Truth Heals", she talks about Energy Drainers. She said, "These are the relationships you must avoid." This is especially true when you're trying to accomplish your goals. Energy Drainers carry unnecessary and critical baggage. I saw how true this was while talking with someone that I'll call "Patty". Even when I tried to convince Patty that her situation would turn out good, she still wanted to believe the worst. So I did what

Deborah advised on her program; I stopped engaging in the conversation. Patty didn't need me; she just wanted to complain, because it felt good to her. Needy relationships will drain you. To maintain healthy relationships, you have to be healthy. Again, it's all about working on you and strengthening your weak traits without excuses.

Authenticity is not insecure. – Once an attractive lady came into my office with her husband to conduct business (so I thought). Her husband had been a customer for over five years. A polite and friendly man, but this was my first time meeting his new wife (of two years). He said, "I wanted her to meet you." Then she said to me, "He's always talking about how wonderful you are." I smiled at the accolades not knowing what I was dealing with ... at first. I was really pleased to meet his wife and tried to start a friendly conversation with her, but she became critical. None of my services were what she needed for new business. She did all the talking and he was not able to say a word after the introduction. My spirit picked up that she was insecure about her husband's relationships around other women. I thought to myself, "I know he catches hell at home." She was attractive but her attitude made her look and act stupid. It was clear she didn't trust her husband. I humorously put in my mind, "Maybe her underwear is too tight" or "Perhaps she is just having a bad day." Whatever the case, I felt no connection to her negative energy. I was in a good mood when they came in, and I was in a good mood when they left. Authenticity is not insecure, envious or selfish. *"There is a little difference in people, but that little difference makes a big difference. The little difference is attitude. The big difference is whether it is positive or negative."* ~W. Clement Stone

Every problem has a solution. — C. Austin Miles a former pharmacist found his *authentic* life as an editor. He wrote *"In the Garden"*, a gospel song published in 1912 that won two Academy Awards in 1984 for the movie "Places in the Heart", starring Sally Fields. In his biography his great-granddaughter said the song, *"In the Garden"* was written in a cold, dreary and leaky basement in New Jersey with no window to let the sun beam in and no view of a garden nearby. But he saw God walking and talking to him in the peaceful and refreshing garden in his mind. In his storm he wrote a master piece of a song. *"After every storm the sun will smile; for every problem there is a solution, and the soul's indefeasible duty is to be of good cheer."* ~William R. Alger.

- The problem is the answer to your dream in disguise.
- Never give up on a problem, because every problem has an answer.

-    Don't wear the problem on your shoulders. Use
     the problem for information.

Set your focus. — Billy Ray Cyrus attended college on
a baseball scholarship. His biography states being a lefty
—he tried playing his father's guitar, but could never learn it.
But that's where he put his focus. His gift was in music and
once he found his true *authentic* self, it helped him to make
history in country music. I also read about Mary J. Blige (one
of the world's greatest and admired singers); it was her focus
that led her from being a hairstylist to that of a sensational
world famous singer and actress. You may not be able to see
the Mary J. Blige in you, but she is a person (like you and I)
who reached for her dreams and kept going until the dream
came true. She found her *authentic* self and it is possible for
everyone to do the same.

Chuck Yeager — Keep being your best. Your body will
"tremble and sweat" as you get closer to your dream coming
forth. The birthing of your dream is like the "cockpit shaking
before breaking the sound barrier." The dream is always
bigger than you imagine and the price is sometimes more than
you want pay. It is recorded that Charles Elwood "Chuck"
Yeager became the first pilot to travel faster than sound;
breaking the sound barrier on October 14, 1947. On the day
of the flight, Yeager was in much pain because he fell from

a horse and broke two ribs two days before the scheduled flight. His dream of making the flight was more intense than the pain in his body. Yeager made the flight and made history. *"You do what you can for as long as you can, and when you finally can't, you do the next best thing. You back up but you don't give up."* ~Chuck Yeager

The keys to staying focused. – Do your best today. Work as if the doors to your dream will open tomorrow. When things look impossible just know everything can change... instantly. Disagree with negative thinking. Your dream will happen because it's your destiny. You have a purpose in life. Stay focused and dream; allow the dream to manifest you into your unlimited *authentic* self. Whisk away boredom by working on your dream and rest your mind from the struggles of life. God works with a purpose. When it was spoken it was done, and when it was done God rested. *"And on the seventh day God ended his work which he had made; and he rested on the seventh day from all his work which he had made."* ~Genesis 2:2

Steve Harvey – One biography said Steve Harvey, comedian, actor, game show host, TV show host, radio personality and author (I'm sure I left out something) once owned a carpet-cleaning company and he sold insurance. And to think... all of these talents embody one man. Steve Harvey isn't some super-human walking the earth; he's a person (like me and you) who once worked his carpet cleaning business while knowing he had another dream inside of him. That's the key word KNOWING … you must know yourself and the dream you embody. *"God lets you be successful because he trusts you that you will do the right thing with it. Now, does he get disappointed often? All the time, because people get there and they forget how they got it."* ~Steve Harvey

Don't forget the dream. − Keep the dream alive by knowing and never forgetting it. While you're at the restaurant washing dishes, at the office pushing paper, serving tables, working hard at the plant or at a dead-end job don't forget the dream! You must give one hundred-percent service to your employer, and work faithfully. As time allows put in the time to work on your dream. If where you are is the place of your destiny, you will be growing and having peace of mind. However, if where you are offers no growth or a peace of mind this is your sign that your life has another purpose. It's a good thing when you're on a job and feeling unfilled because this is your indication … don't forget the dream.

Johnny Allen Hendrix — I love watching the Biography Channel because I look at success stories as motivation and the tragic endings as warnings. I read about Jimi Hendrix and it's noted that he's the greatest electric guitarist in the history of rock music. Based on his childhood, Johnny Allen Hendrix (Jimi Hendrix) the successful guitarist, singer and songwriter, was never meant to be. There was so much pain, sickness, early death of family members, separation from siblings and being forced into adulthood while he was still a child. Such sad beginnings, but amazingly he used his guitar to find his *authentic* success. His talents made room for him to do major interviews, receive awards and triumph beyond measures. It is also noted that he played and recorded with Little Richard's band in the 60's. Jimi was quoted saying, *"I want to do with my guitar what Little Richard does with his voice."* Jimi Hendrix became a household name. Sorrowfully, at the age of twenty-seven he was dead. The moral of the story is success happens when you put forth the effort; how long the success lasts is up to you.

You may be an unknown. — Marilyn McCoo and Billy Davis, Jr.'s soulful song, *"You Don't Have to Be Star"*, says exactly what I'm saying in terms of being unknown on the celebrity list, but living in your community with purpose and passion. Highly respected and known in the part of the world where you are called to inspire and change:

Dr. Charles Davis — I spoke with Drs. Charles and Georgia Davis, founders of The BBC School of Theology as they prepared for the first graduating class. Dr. Charles

Davis told me that while he worked most of his life for a major airline, he also worked diligently in his church and never forsook the dream to have his own ministry. The theology school was birthed out of his labor to stay focused on his dream.

Pastor J.D. Walker — Pastor Walker preaches many wonderful sermons at Mt. Pleasant Missionary Baptist Church in my hometown Woodbury, Georgia; touching the hearts of so many with his wisdom of the bible. Even when he worked a 9 to 5 job to support his family, he still preached at the church and served the community in the same uplifting spirit.

Bishop Thomas Daniel — Bishop Daniel also has a power church and outreach ministry in my hometown of Woodbury (Woodbury Miracle Center). The church needed someone with a powerful vision to continue the dream of the founder (Pastor Bowles), and Bishop Daniel went above and beyond in the development of the church and the community.

Drs. Jonathon and Sylvia Carter — This powerful ministry couple have personally given me so much love and support on my journey. They believe in building leaders. Pastors of Siloam International (College Park, Georgia) Drs. Jonathon and Sylvia Carter are superstars in their own rights to everyone who knows them.

Authentic Relationships

Chapter 12:

The person walking this mission with you must be an asset and not a liability. Like a plant, the relationship should grow and produce. *Authentic* relationships are dream makers; even if the partnership dissolves the dream lives on. *Authentic* relationships are like iron sharpening iron and in love with birthing the dream.

"We were given:

> *Two hands to hold.*
> *To legs to walk.*
> *Two eyes to see.*
> *Two ears to listen.*
> *But why only one heart?*
> *Because the other was given to someone else.*
> *For us to find."*

-Unknown

Boaz and Ruth — Ruth's first husband died. She was living in a strange country with her mother-in-law and they were both widowers. Ruth didn't have any skills and didn't know anyone except her mother- in-law. However, Ruth didn't sit back and cry, "Poor me." She got up and looked for work to support the two of them. The point is to work diligently where you are; this is the road to success. Ruth's first job in her new town was field work. She wasn't too proud to work in the field. That particular field held the key to her future and it changed her life forever. As she worked in the field, Boaz diligently observed her and was impressed with what he saw. Soon thereafter, a relationship between the two of them developed. This union gave Ruth a second chance to live her *authentic* life. She moved from being a poor and broke field worker to the wife of Boaz, the rich field owner. This union chronicled them in history as the grandparents of King David.

Desi Arnez and Lucille Ball — The young and old generations remember Desi Arnez and Lucille Ball, creators of "I Love Lucy" and founders of Desilu Productions. They are credited as the inventors of the reruns in connection with their TV show which opened doors for other networks. They had it all (success, money, thriving business in the movie industry, and a beautiful family), but the marriage collapsed. Nevertheless, what they did together in business, television and movies lives on forever. The output of a powerful *authentic* relationship lives on even if the union ends.

Will and Jada Smith — The power that Will and Jada Smith have as a couple is obvious. It is said they first met when she auditioned for the role of Smith's girlfriend on his series, "The Fresh Prince of Bel-Air." She was not selected for the role because she was considered too short for the part, but as fate would have it—they eventually got married. That is why you should never believe the press; what others say you can or cannot do (or have). The accomplishments of Will and Jada Smith are amazing. Sure they've had their share of rumors; but they've proven what happens when two minds think in agreement about success, becoming more successful in their *authentic* calling; acting, producing, writing and making a powerful family.

Bishop T.D. and Serita Jakes — "Get Ready! Get Ready! Get Ready!" (Famous words from Bishop Jakes). Bishop T.D. and Serita Jakes are a powerful ministry team who established The Potter's House, Woman Thou Art Loose, Man Power, and a variety of movies, "Jumping the Broom" and "Sparkle" (Whitney Houston's last performance), just to name a few. This couple is inspiring, successful and world leaders. But as Gladys Knight's song says, *"They had their share of ups and downs."* Their biography is full of family tragedies, early poverty, and hardships. They are proof that God will turn it all around if you keep doing your part (keep believing). I remember when Bishop Jakes preached a message on "God's Timing". He spoke with great conviction because he had already walked through what he preached and that made it a reality.

Johnny and Vondala Lyles — Let go of the thoughts regarding how, when and where you will meet your *authentic* partner. Your timing is in the creation of life. Many couples met by a chance encounter. My friend Vondala and her husband Johnny met on the expressway after they both experienced a flat tire at the same time ...they got married and started a T-Shirt line called, "UCDAT" (U Can Do All Things).

Robert Levine and Mary Tyler Moore — Just what the doctor ordered. One of my favorite actresses, Mary Tyler Moore (not only an outstanding actress, but an active individual in charity work and various political causes, particularly around the issues of animal rights and Diabetes) met her husband (who is a doctor and seventeen years her junior) when her mother was his patient and being treated by him. When it's meant to happen... it will.

Kevin Hunter, Sr. and Wendy Williams Hunter — Talk show host, actress and author Wendy Williams' (How you doin'?) second husband, Kevin became her agent. Personally,

I believe when your partner works with you in the business it takes some of the load off your shoulders and makes you a more effective partner. Wendy is definitely a powerful woman on the move and is benefiting from the *authentic* agent in her *authentic* life.

George and Ira Gershwin — Magical Relationship. Power couples are not always married. They are together based on the vision and mission. They need each other's *authentic* energy. They are male and female, male and male or female and female. Case and point, George and Ira Gershwin (brothers) were successful musical composers. George died when he was only thirty-eight, but he along with his brother gave the world hundreds of beautiful compositions: *"Rhapsody in Blue, An American in Paris, Porgy and Bess, and They Can't Take That Away from Me"*. to name a few.

Fred Astaire and Ginger Rogers — In the movie, *"Can We Dance"* Fred Astaire song *"They can't take that away from me"* (George and Ira Gershwin's song) to his powerful dance partner Ginger Rogers. Astaire and Rogers were only acting partners. They had the right chemistry when they worked together and ten movies came out of their partnership. *Authentic* relationships look like that of lovers; they are together because they are with one mind to get great things accomplished.

Love is where you find it. — I found so many couples shaping the world that I couldn't list all them all. *Authentic* couples are defined by purpose. I asked my nephew Jordan Goodwin (who was eighteen at the time) about his thoughts regarding a younger man marrying a much older woman, or an older man marrying a much younger woman. He simply said, "Love is where you find it." A blueprint doesn't exist for *authentic* couples. They are who they are regardless of height, weight, age and gender; they are powerful in getting things done. Desi Arnez and Lucille Ball changed the world with their talents, and for that they were *authentic.* When you know God is not a respecter of persons ... as you observe Bishop Jakes, the Smiths, and the Lyles and other *authentic* relationships making dreams happen, you should be confident that your dreams will come true too. It would be wonderful if every magical relationship lasted forever. Some do – some don't. "They last as long as they last". Whether they remain a couple, friends or foes their *authentic* talents cannot be denied. Somehow their dreams are purposed to service the world with bliss. As the song says, *"You can't take that away (from them)."*

Dreams Do Come True

Chapter 13:

My friend Sharon (Ladee Storem) Acres is a playwright. People call her the "female" Tyler Perry. Her first play was *I Love My Man More Than God* and her second play was *Lord Turn This Hell House Into A Home.* Both were really funny. I attended each play because I'm supportive of her work. I like the fire in Sharon. She constantly fuels her dreams with the desire to be an *authentic* person. One minute she's building her cleaning business; the next she's receiving accolades for the plays she write. She is living proof, "where there's a will, there's a way". She stayed with the plan and she will soon be listed among the great actors, directors, playwrights, screenwriters and producers ... why not? Isn't that how it works? Perseverance and faith are in the wings working on a bigger plan. When you sincerely want all that life has to offer — you put in the time. *"Put your heart, mind, intellect and soul even to your smallest acts. This is the secret of success."* ~Swami Sivananda

Stay with the Plan. – When you stay with the plan, you will one day experience the authenticity of the dream. People may not see who you are right now and to them perhaps you're just the "average Joe" or "plain Jane". Keep living your dream and remember that your next door neighbor could be the next Steve Jobs; the store clerk that assists you may become a Katie Couric; or the handyman that works on your repairs could be Jamie Foxx in the making. I have many *authentic* friends, who are successful in their own right, and one day you will hear and read more about them; *Poets like*: Adrienne Prather, Ozzie James, James Hayes, Harry Richardson and Milton Graves. *Talents beyond measure like*: Aaron Lamont Slaton, a composer; Jordan Goodwin, a computer whiz; Zayreton Slaton, a musical sensation; Kerry Whitehead, another Kirk Franklin; Erus Davenport, a motivational speaker; Resha Jones, an opera singer; and Clinton Nicholas, a fitness gurus. *Successful business men and women like:* Wesley Benjamin, Shawn Brooks, Cleveland Clements, Sonya Wright, Shelia Riddle Traylor, Danny Hayes, G. Fabre, Alvin and Sharon Crouch, Larry and Ken McNealey, Nigel Soares, Richard Chestnut, Roger Anthony, T. Brown, Peter Seow, Fred Walker, Cedric Shepherd, Tameka S. Sykes, Nelson and Cynthia Okolo and Alvin and Paulette (Staley) Reynolds. They are unknown talents (for right now); yet they are still living their *authentic* dream and blossoming where they are planted.

Diana Ross — An array of the finest actors and singers starred in the well renown film, *"The Wiz"*: Diana Ross, Michael Jackson, Nipsey Russell, Ted Ross, Mabel King, Theresa Merritt, Thelma Carpenter, Lena Horne and Richard Pryor. This movie is so much fun to watch and Diana Ross' voice electrifies the song "Home". It is said that initially the (teenager at that time) R&B singer Stephanie Mills, who originated the role on Broadway — was to be cast as Dorothy. Ross, in her thirties at the time was said to be too old for the part, but remarkably she pulled it off. I loved Diana Ross in this role … she did an amazing job. It was stated by Pauline Kael, a film critic, *"Ross' effort to get the film into production is perhaps the strongest example of sheer will in film history."* That is exactly what's needed to pull off your dream, "sheer will". As it stands the role was destined for Ms. Ross and she still had to — (you still have to) knock at the door with sheer will.

The dream will happen. – I heard about an author who had a problem getting his work published. With one final attempt, he wrote what he felt was his best work; however, it was rejected by the publishers. The lack of success in getting his book published led him into a great and eventually he committed suicide. After his death his family had the manuscript printed in his memory. This time the book caught the eye of another publisher and became a bestseller. Many give up too soon, not realizing how close they are to their dreams coming to realization. When the trial gets unbearable and people turn against you, this is your sign that good things are coming your way.

Lewis and Clark — To survive life, you must live your *authentic* dream! Every history student should remember the explorers "Lewis and Clark". Lewis Meriwether and William Clark were explorers and soldiers, and their mission was to explore the territory of the Louisiana Purchase. The expedition laid much of the groundwork for the westward expansion of the United States. Lewis Meriwether was a skilled hunter and outdoorsman, but after his (dream) job ended as an explorer he was assigned to work as a public administrator. It is said that Meriwether committed suicide at the age of 35. Someone commenting on his death said, "He was placed on a job that was outside of his element, as an explorer and outdoorsman". We were born to live a certain dream and nothing else can quench that thirst. Once William Clark married he named one of his sons Meriwether, after his late-friend and expedition partner. The moral of the story is the same; you must stay with your heart's passion and be your *authentic* self.

Live your dreams anyway. — I heard this story about a man who studied to be a doctor, because this is what his parents wanted him to do. He was often depressed because his heart was not in his studies. During a counseling session for his depression, the counselor concluded that his real problem was dissatisfaction in his career choice. The counselor asked, "What do you like doing?" As a child, the young man remembered the enjoyment of going to the hardware store and watching the owner interact with his customers while he worked. Subconsciously, he wanted to one day own a hardware store. As he got ready for college, his family wanted him to follow in his father and older brother's career path (in the medical field). To his dissatisfaction, he was living the dream that his family dreamed for him, and not the dream that he dreamed for himself. After counseling, the young man followed his heart and eventually opened his own hardware store. He was instantly cured from depression. It's important for you to be true to yourself and live your dream. Some people must see the success of the dream before they can believe in the dream. That is why you must hold true to the passion of your heart and live your life's calling.

Do what you love. — Your *authentic* job looks effortless to others. Family and friends consider your talent as a mere hobby. When the money is slow coming in they might say to you, "Get a real job." Yet you are willing to sacrifice because your *authentic* job brings your heart indisputable joy. Life is too short to do things you hate every day (forever). Someone once said there are two important days in a person's life, "the day they are born" and "the day they discover WHY they were born!" It's wise to take time to seek out your heart's desire and put effort into seeing your dreams fulfilled. Doing what you love doesn't come easily. You have to work the plan and plan the work until it takes form. The work of authors such as Stephen King, William Golding, Anne Frank and J.K. Rowling was rejected. Since they didn't give up, their body of work touched the world. Many starving writers, aspiring actors and beginning singers are turned away without hope of a chance. Follow your heart. Listen to your spirit. Live and stay with the plan; the money will soon follow. *"The best revenge is massive success."* ~Frank Sinatra

Jack Canfield — Our soul needs soul prosperity and tender love and care in order to prosper in hard times. Hard times could mean the boss calls you into the office and gives you the pink slip, your house is in foreclosure, your business is going under or the doctor gives you or a love one a bad report. Then more things happen, the car needs repairing, the money is not available and the bank account is in the hot red. I am talking about hard times hitting you left and right. Motivational speakers Jack Canfield and Mark Victor Hansen compiled a series of books called *"Chicken Soup for the Soul"*. The series of books feature a collection of short stories with inspirational messages. It makes you think of reclining in your easy chair after one of those tough days with a relaxing cup of your favorite hot soup or tea. This book pampers the soul back to good health and gives your mind a break from thinking of hard times. At end of *"Chicken Soup for the Soul"* stories, there is help for the helpless, love for the unloved and a solution for the problem. So, while you're in a posture of relaxing and pampering the soul, play some easy to listen to music, and meditate on the positive outcome you expect to receive because hard times won't last forever.

Good soil. – One day my brother shared with me a load of life's problems. He noticed that I was composed as he shared these problems and I calmly responded, "It will all work out." He asked, "Why are you so calm?" I replied, "Worrying and getting upset will not change anything." I stood on the good soil of faith, which says that "all things work together for the good to those who love the Lord." Another time, I spoke with a person who shared with me all the things he did to make his circle of friends happy. I thought to myself, "This has to be draining" because people who are for you don't take you through unnecessary changes.

When you have done all that you can do learn how to stand and discover your *authentic* self.

Rich soil grows a rich life. – I'm sharing these wisdom nuggets with you because you need to plant your time, thoughts and conversations in good soil (people). Sometimes you can get lost in the bad situations of life and other people's problems. People will try to make their problems – your problems. Secondhand problems are like secondhand smoke…dangerous to your life and to your dream because problems can leave you helpless. These problems are not about you and your dream. Make every attempt to find the good soil and enjoy your life. When your thoughts are not congested, blessings can come from the north, south, east and west. The *authentic* life is about thinking prosperity, speaking prosperity and living prosperous. *"Beloved, I wish above all things that thou mayest prosper and be in health, even as thy soul prospereth."* ~ (3 John 1:2, KJV)

Late Bloomers

Chapter 14:

The alarm for achieving your goal goes off in your mind like the early morning alarm clock. You are looking at life as though you've entered into the "Twilight Zone". You can almost hear Rod Serling say "Sorry... your age has terminated your dream." Wake-up! It's not a dream come true. As you get older, you may feel the rush in your mind saying, "Your goals cannot be reached." Fret not! Your dream is still on a tangible plane that's waiting to land. You are just in the ranks with the "late bloomers".

The meaning of late bloomers. — The late bloomers are the people who use their gifts later in life. They do away with the "It's too late" excuse and develop a "better late than never" attitude. The late bloomers have the same success (if not more) as their younger counterparts. By gaining wisdom from past experiences, they have an ageless and powerful will to accomplish greatness...NOW.

Confession of a late bloomer. — I can relate to anyone who is a late bloomer. When I became a business owner in my late thirties most of my new friends (networking with me) were younger. Sure, I wish I could have started earlier, but that wasn't my life. During the years of not living in my purpose, I accepted my life as it was. Like most people, I allowed that time to define me. However, (like most dreamers) I couldn't deny the need for more. Neither age nor the length of time it would take for me to accomplish my dream was my focus anymore because I became consumed with passion for the dream. Of course, the detractors were there to remind me, "You are too old." But, the mission blindsided me and I could no longer hear the critics. As I look back over my life, I realize I was on schedule with my life's calling. Starting later in life (doing what I had do in spite of age) prepared me for this place and time. Encourage others so they won't quit. Like Frances, a new friend who entered my path after reading my first book *Fabulous Over Forty,* said she kept the book on her nightstand right next to her bible. (What an honor). Moreover, she told me how the book encouraged her to feel good about getting older. She didn't want to feel like an old woman when she had an ageless mindset. Frances is living her *authentic* life.

Late bloomers making it happen. — I was talking with Carol, who got married (for the first time) in her forties. She said she never voiced negative thoughts about meeting "Mr. Right." She kept her words positive, and had steadfast faith that her husband was in her future. Carol said she lived uncluttered in her mind and lifestyle. The moral behind Carol's story is to stay ready for unanswered prayers to be answered. Carol advised, "It's better to be ready than to try and get ready." Like the parable in the bible about the "Ten Virgins," five were wise and five were foolish. The ten virgins were going out on a journey to meet the bridegroom. The five wise virgins took extra oil for the trip, but the five foolish did not. The five wise virgins with extra oil were ready to complete the journey, but the five foolish were left in the dark. Late bloomers should stay ready for their opportunities. *"Sometimes opportunity knocks, but most of the time it sneaks up and then quietly steals away."* ~Doug Larson

Starting where you are. — Many late bloomers began living their *authentic* dream after retirement from a major company; some after raising their children (grandchildren); and others went back to school (later in life) to get more up-to-date training for a new career. Perhaps late bloomers are "late bloomers" because they were not ready (for one reason or another) for the quest of their dream. (Achieving success at the wrong time can be destructive). Living the dream is not about age; it's about readiness. Late bloomers (I read and believe) are deep thinkers and the "*authentic* late bloomers" refuses to miss out on their opportunities. The late bloomers have time to gather valuable knowledge to do astonishing tasks in the world and pass on the knowledge to others. They are influential in life because they make a difference. Salma Hayek was born1966. Her career as an actress took notice in her twenties. In her thirties leading up to her forties, she founded her own film production company, became the spokesperson for Avon cosmetics, married French billionaire and PPR CEO Francois-Henri Pinault, gave birth to her daughter, started her own line of cosmetics and her accomplishments continue to increase. Ms. Hayek is a late bloomer, but she understands that age does not stop the *authentic* late bloomers from reaching their successful place in life. *"I'll tell you, there is nothing better in life than being a late bloomer. I believe that success can happen at any time and at any age."* ~Salma Hayek

Late Bloomers must protect their (authentic) identity. — Walking through the pathway of life you will be someone's husband or wife, father or mother, son or daughter, brother or sister, uncle or aunt, grandparent, cousin and so on. Some people only know you by titles, and others still don't know your real name. They refer to you as "old school" and load you down with (although respectful) too many "Yes mams" and "No sirs". They call you "mama" yet, they're not your child. Strangers ask, "What's up pop?" You are a full-grown woman or man still being called by a nickname that you had in the first grade ("Lil'Bit, June-bug, Pee-wee, Stinky, Chicken-head, Piggy or Pudding"…). Your spirit is still young and ready for new dreams. However, some delights in addressing you as though you are that same old person they labeled "way-back when". Some even believes it's their place to put you with the "over-the-hill-gang" without a "get out of jail free pass". Thank God others do not negate your destiny. You are the exception to the rules, and you can free yourself from the titles and the labels by living your *authentic* life.

The authentic life for the late bloomers. — The first thing the late bloomers must do is start the process of shedding away the layers:

- Shame of the past.
- Holding on to mistakes.
- Mistrust.
- Anger and bitterness.

The layers are keeping the late bloomers from pressing toward the mark of their high calling. I know of a very talented man who was once an excellent cook. There was a time he talked about cooking and you could see a spark light up in his eyes. (He should have had his own cooking show). I saw him recently but his spark for cooking was gone. He allowed the wrong people to tell him he was too old and that he was foolish to think he could make a living as a chef. As we continued to talk, he didn't talk about cooking; instead he complained about life. This is what happens when you lose your passion to live your dream. The *authentic* life is about living with passion and not allowing anyone or anything to rob the *authentic* dream inside of you. The late bloomers' passion does not die with age, instead it is birthed:

Mary Kay a famous late bloomer. — She was forty-five when she started Mary Kay Cosmetics. *"Most people live and die with their music still not played. They never dare to try."* ~Mary Kay Ash

John Glenn a famous late bloomer. — He was forty-one when he first orbited the Earth in 1962. At the age of seventy-seven he became the oldest person to fly in space, and the only one to fly in both the Mercury and Shuttle programs. *"I suppose the one quality in an astronaut more powerful than any other is curiosity. They have to get some place nobody's ever been."* ~John Glenn

Hank Aaron a famous late bloomer. — He was forty when he hit his 715th home run. *"I don't want them to forget Babe Ruth. I just want them to remember me!"* ~Hank Aaron

Julia Child a famous late bloomer. — She collaborated on her first French cooking book when she was just months shy of her 50th birthday*." I was 32 when I started cooking; up until then, I just ate."* ~Julia Child

Sylvester Stallone a famous late bloomer. — He was thirty years old when he wrote and starred in the first movie *Rocky*; when he was forty three years old he developed the movie *Rambo*.

George Foreman a famous late bloomer. — He recaptured the heavyweight championship with a 10th round knockout, becoming the oldest person ever to win the heavyweight championship. *"The question isn't at what age I want to retire, it's at what income."* ~George Foreman

Grandma Moses a famous late bloomer. — She was a renowned American folk artist in her seventies when she started painting scenes of her rural life in upstate New York. "Life is what we make it, always has been, always will be." ~Anna Mary Robertson Moses better known as "Grandma Moses"

Colonel Sanders a famous late bloomer. — His fame had a complicated start in life but he realized he had an original cooking talent. It was not until he was in his sixties that he started his business and became a millionaire. *"There's no reason to be the richest man in the cemetery. You can't do any business from there."* ~Colonel Sanders of finger lickin' good chicken, Kentucky Fried Chicken.

Laura Elizabeth Ingalls Wilders a famous late bloomer. — She was an American author who wrote the "Little House" series of books based on her childhood experience in a pioneer family. She published her first book at the age of sixty-five. "The Little House on the Prairie" television series aired 1974 and was based on her book. *"Every job is good if you do your best and work hard. A man who works hard stinks only to the ones that have nothing to do but smell."* ~Laura Elizabeth Ingalls Wilder

Ray Kroc a famous late bloomer. — He was in his fifties when he achieved success in the restaurant business. *"The two most important requirements for major success are: first, being in the right place at the right time, and second, doing something about it."* ~Ray Kroc, Principal Establisher of the McDonald's Corporation

Wally Amos was a famous late bloomer. — He was in his forties when he started his famous Cookie Company. *"Nothing is an obstacle unless you say it is."* ~ Wally Amos (Famous Amos)

Don't Despise Small Beginnings

Chapter 15:

In their biographies it speaks about the humbling and sometimes strange jobs that successful people held before finding their *authentic* calling:

Don't despise small beginnings — I read that author and motivational speaker, Zig Ziglar (See You At The Top) started out as a salesman, and was in his fifties when his books and motivational speaking took off.

Don't despise small beginnings — The chairman of Dell Computer, Michael Dell earned $2.50 an hour washing dishes at a Chinese restaurant.

Don't despise small beginnings — Actor Hugh Jackman was once a party clown.

Don't despise small beginnings — Before Larry Holmes became a professional boxer and businessman, he drove a dump truck.

Don't despise small beginnings — Actor Matthew McConaughey was a chicken coop cleaner.

Don't despise small beginnings — Talk show host and comedian Ellen DeGeneres once worked as a house painter, waitress, sales clerk and an oyster shucker.

Don't despise small beginnings — The Rock and Roll Hall of Famer (singing artist) Rod Stewart was once a gravedigger.

Don't despise small beginnings — "Rocky's" actor, screenwriter and director, Sylvester Stallone was once a lion cage cleaner.

Don't despise small beginnings — Rapper, record producer, entrepreneur and actor, Sean "Diddy" Combs was a paperboy.

Don't despise small beginnings — Singer, actress and dancer, Jennifer Lopez worked as a legal assistant.

Don't despise small beginnings — Academy Award winner, actor, director, writer and diplomat Sidney Poitier held a string of jobs as a dishwasher.

Don't despise small beginnings — Singer Mariah Carey was a hat checker.

Don't despise small beginnings — Singer, actor, and film producer, "The Material Girl," Madonna once worked at Dunkin Donuts.

Don't despise small beginnings — The life of successful people didn't just happen on a bed of roses; they persevered and made the dream happen anyway! They worked various jobs to make a living (but they didn't forget their dream). Matthew McConaughey is quoted saying, *"Those types of trips are really the ones that leave a lasting impression."*

Appreciate the journey. — Remember, it only takes a second for your life to change. People have found overnight success —overnight. Time is precious so don't waste it. When you want to live your *authentic* life, you must use every minute wisely. Appreciate every day knowing it's an honor to be alive, because some people didn't live to see it. The bible says, "One day with the Lord is like a thousand years, and a thousand years as one day." As I read and wrote about the people profiled in this book, it became clearer in how God's plans unfolded to those who were ready. Life is not a free ride. You must be ready for action. A dreamer must be a doer of the dream; they need a plan of action when it's time, and they can't despise the small beginnings. *"I have learned that if one advances confidently in the direction of his dreams, and endeavors to live the life he has imagined, he will meet with a success unexpected in common hours."* ~Henry David Thoreau

It's Not Too Late

Chapter 16:

There was a time in your life when the pursuit of your future was written down in your high school yearbook and your life's path was given devoted consideration. It was in your plans to get a college degree, start your career, do some traveling, and then (maybe) start a family. How wrong you were! Your life has been nothing like you wrote or thought it to be:

The Twenties — You knew for sure the twenties would last forever. You were young, cute and adventurous; having the time of your life. You thought you knew more than your parents and you had a "made-up mind" (doing it your way).

The Thirties — You couldn't believe it … life took you on a (totally) different path. You didn't finish college, you didn't expect the child (without a marriage), and you wanted to travel the world, but you ended up working day and night (just) to make ends meet.

The Forties — You decided to move to a new city and start-over. In the midst of your new life you got a divorce. The family grew, yet your income stayed the same. To make matters worse you are overweight, have high blood pressure, and you're full of regrets and stress.

The Fifties — NOW, you are ready to hear somebody (anybody) give you a word of wisdom. This is the story of many older women and men, who still have young unfinished dreams. The word is "it's not over... it's to be continued." Diana Ross sings, *"Do You Know Where You Are Going To?"*... So take the time to know where you are going by listening to your *authentic* calling.

Lessons of life. — Some of the above situations "may or may not" fit your life, but if you are feel unfulfilled (in anyway) keep reading. The time to plan for life is once you find your *authentic* self. If you are "not" looking within then you're looking for life in all the wrong places. Before you can make logic out of where you are right now the question, "What are you here to do?" must be understood, answered, and then executed. As noted in an earlier chapter, "you may be doing other things before getting on the right path of life, but don't forget your dream".

It will come to pass. — "Surprise! Surprise! Surprise!" as the character Gomer Pyle would say. Now is the time to take out the formal dress, and get the tuxedo cleaned (it may need a few alterations) because it's your time to dance, sing and do YOU! You may not be able to do the goals you wrote down in the high school year book, but you "can do" what's in your heart NOW. This is your season and you're at the right age to discover your *authentic* self; it starts where you are … right now!

Isabelle King — My friend Isabelle "Isy" King shared how at an early age she loved to draw and paint, but she was always too busy raising a family and working jobs to make a living, as a result of life she discontinued her painting. However, in her sixties, Isy picked up her brushes to start painting again. She did a lovely portrait of me, which I proudly display in my office. Painting is her *authentic* dream and she did not let it die.

Count your moments and not your months. — At age sixty, Rabindranath Tagore a poet, author and lecturer (born in Calcutta) took up drawing and painting; successful exhibitions of his many works were held throughout Europe. Moreover, many successful people counted the moments and not the months:

- Vera Wang started designing wedding gowns at age 40, becoming a famous and lucrative fashion designer.

- Leonard Cohen started his career as a poet in Canada, but he was in his 30s when he released his first album, *Songs of Leonard Cohen*, which was a masterpiece.

- Hillary Clinton definitely count the moments and not the months. She was a First Lady of Arkansas, a First Lady of the United States, a Senator (New York), a lead candidate for the Democratic presidential nomination, she served as the 67th United States Secretary of States when she was in her 60s, and there's a possibility that she may run for the U.S. president in 2016; she is an *authentic* high achiever. She can do it all and you can do it all too. Rabindranath Tagore quoted, *"The butterfly counts not months but moments, and has time enough."*

You never know. — Every person on earth is here for a reason and a season of life. Recently, I met a very inspiring woman who told me the story of how she entered college in her forties. Her (teenage) classmates called her "the old lady". She said, "It was tough being the oldest person in the classroom." Nevertheless, she didn't let the comments about her age stop her from pursuing her degree or from becoming the smartest student in the class. Today, at the age of forty-seven she is a fifth grade teacher who is still pursuing more dreams. She is an *authentic* person. That is how life is, the moment you connect with your *authentic* dreams, other dreams will follow.

Live your passion. – In my Fabulous over Forty Networking group there are ladies in their forties and fifties completing college: Pam Martin, Janice Cliatt and Laura Minor to name a few. I have a customer name Arthur Boykin (I call him Ace) launching his *authentic* career; he drives a cab, but his passion is to be a community activist. He loves talking with others about coming together and making their neighborhood safe. One day Ace stepped out "on the limb" by purchasing items he needed for the dream (I tell everyone, you need a seed). He started by having his slogan designed, T-Shirts made, brochures and flyers printed, and a CD of his recorded message. Arthur (Ace) Boykin is ready to demonstrate his *authentic* life. Dreams are ready when you are but sometimes you may have to go out on a limb. The bible document these words spoken to the Prophet Habakkuk from the Lord, *"For the vision (dream) is yet for the appointed time, but at the end it shall speak, and not lie; though it tarry, wait for it; because it will surely come and not tarry."*

Claim your dreams. — Pursue your dreams. See yourself accomplishing unfinished goals. Mr. Danner, a friend of a friend shared with me that he retired from a high profile position at a major company now the job was over and he felt lost. The job had consumed his life. At sixty-three, he felt that he didn't have anything left to do, but join the senior citizen center. However, there were still unfulfilled dreams inside of him. Finally, he decided to pursue his (lifelong) passion by taking money from his savings and starting a small computer training center. The poet, Tagore said, *"Age considers; youth ventures."* When you continue to live your dreams you are ageless. Be like Caleb (who followed Moses); he would not allow his age to stop him from claiming his promises. Caleb's words to Joshua were, *"Now, as you can see, the Lord has kept me alive and well as he promised for all these forty-five years...Today I am eighty-five years old. I am as strong now as I was when Moses sent me on that journey, and I can still travel and fight as well as I could then. So give me the hill country that the Lord promised me."* ~ (Joshua 14:10-12, NLT)

A Personal Testimony. — My personal testimony is similar to the woman who was the oldest person in the classroom. When I was in my thirties, I went back to school to study Commercial Art. My drive to be happy in a career motivated me to finish art school. When I was in my forties I received training to become a certified aerobics instructor; again, I was the oldest student in the class. Nevertheless, I became one of the best aerobics instructors at the health club (so I was told). Life starts where you are; if you could have done the dream earlier ... you would have done it. You have to appreciate "who" you are and "where" you are NOW. Never stop dreaming and never lose the passion to follow your *authentic* dream at every age and stage of life.

Staying Authentic

Chapter 17:

What is your *authentic* life's calling? Without answering this question, you will find yourself going around in circles. However, when you discover your calling, the reason for your existence becomes meaningful. The way to know your *authentic* calling is to follow your gut-feeling (also called: your inner spirit, instinct and intuition). Tyler Perry calls it "listening to your life". To find and live your *authentic* calling:

1. Believe God has a plan for you.

2. Listen to your life.

3. Develop what you enjoy doing.

4. Find friends who support you.

Discover your life's calling. — The moment you discover your *authentic* calling, life takes on a new meaning, and you will start looking for ways to make your life better, even in the difficult times. Once you satisfy the question, you will have a peace of mind because you'll know that the obligation of your calling "being fruitful in life" — is in the hands of God. Be what others said you couldn't be and to do what others said you couldn't do. Be all that you are here to be ... don't quit. Your *authentic* life will take you to higher heights and to a richer life. When you are conscious of your *authentic* life, your living is not in vain, and dreaming the impossible dream is not impossible. *"You are not here merely to make a living. You are here in order to enable the world to live more abundantly, with greater vision, and with a finer spirit of hope and achievement. You are here to enrich the world, and you impoverish yourself if you forget the errand."* ~Woodrow Wilson

Don't let the problems blindside you. — Stay alert and do not allow problems to blindside your vision; the plans are not working, the bottom falls out, things gets worst, and the people closest to you begin to act funny. The dilemmas can leave you temporarily stressed and depressed. Before you throw up your hands or jump off the bridge... you must remember that it's only a test. There is a way to get through the calamities and remain *authentic.* The tests will make you stronger to match the blessings coming your way. Big dreamers have big problems, and bigger blessings. Your *authentic* dream is your consoler, and staying with the dream will keep you in the "plastic bubble".

Be focused on the dream. — Instead of focusing on the problem replace it with refocusing on your dream. Talking about the problem will not change it. Replace hopelessness with faith in your dream. What you know for sure is— things have worked-out before, and they will work-out again. The setback is not your finale. Don't spend time trying to figure how the problems will work-out; there are so many ways for the answer to come, and thinking about it will over-work your mind. Remember, your past victories are indicators that everything will end soon and with a positive outcome. Your tears and sadness will fade away and there will be "joy in the morning."

It's about growth. — The *authentic* life is for the strong warriors (the eagles) and not the chickens. The eagles are powerfully built (the *authentic* self), and ready for the challenges of life. Your desires should be to live your life at its highest existence. If you lose focus on your purpose you can easily become complacent. Recently, I researched the biography of an actor to see if he is still living. He was once a well-known famous actor. I read after making his fortune he withdrew from show business, and moved to a ranch out of public view. He was still living, but not active in any causes. It is not a crime to retire and do nothing, I just believe "to whom much is given — much is required." Eleanor Roosevelt said it best, *"I could not at any age be content to take my place in a corner by the fireside and simply look on."*

Authentic love. – Making money is not the end of success. Money to success is like gasoline to a car — getting you from one place to the next. Money can't buy *authentic* love, and success without money will not live to tell the story. *Authentic* dreamers with high standards do not say, "Me, my four and no more." They walk-in love and use their success and money to help others. Diane Latiker is a perfect example of *authentic* love. In 2003, she opened her home in the Chicago South Side area to the neighborhood youth. She started *Founder of Kids Off the Block, a* nonprofit organization dedicated to providing at-risk and low-income youth, a positive alternative to drugs, gangs and violence. She started with 10 kids and it was reported that since opening, the organization has experienced tremendous growth. CNN, BET Awards and many other media outlets have recognized Ms. Latiker's work and labor of love for the youth. Diane Latiker is showing *authentic* love.

Authentic lovers. — The *authentic* lovers don't complain about how bad things are, but they willingly roll up their sleeves, and make a change happen:

- Sandra Bullock helped to rebuild New Orleans after hurricane Katrina.

- George Clooney arranged a huge celebrity-packed telethon to raise funds for the people of Haiti.
- Bono works all over the world, especially in Africa helping the poor and suffering.
- Oprah provides grants to people and nonprofits that do good works in the world.
- Denzel Washington gives donations to the Save Africa's Children and the Boys, Fisher House Foundation and Girls Club.

The unselfish dreamers have big hearts, and a vision to build and pave the way for others. They perform astonishing tasks in the world. *"Great minds discuss ideas; average minds discuss events; small minds discuss people."* ~Eleanor Roosevelt

Stanley Kirk Burrell — Wisdom is the principal thing. A wise man will learn from his mistakes, and become even stronger, as with the story of Stanley Kirk Burrell (better known as M.C. Hammer). He is considered a forefather and pioneer of pop rap, but with all of his accomplishments it was reported that M.C. Hammer had battles with debt and lawsuits (reportedly the 90's rap icon lost his fortune). However, M.C. Hammer was a wise and savvy man; he reestablished himself by undertaking new projects using the

social media to capitalize on his existing personal brand, and by becoming an investor in several tech companies. He appeared on the Oprah Winfrey Show (before OWN) and discussed his involvement in the world of the internet ... through wisdom an *authentic* life can be restored. *"I plan on continuing to explore all the possibilities of technology, and then finally film and television and movies. Embrace it."*
~M.C. Hammer

Cathy Hughes is leading the way. — Cathy Hughes the founder of Radio One has a miraculous story. She was dealing with being divorced, experiencing problems with her employees, financial difficulties, and subsequently losing her home. There was a time when she lived at the radio station with her young son before her life changing moment occurred. Her fortune began to change when she revamped the R&B station to a 24-hour talk radio format. Cathy Hughes founded the media company Radio One and later expanded into TV One. (I firmly believe you must walk in another person's shoes if you want to know the secret to his or her success). Cathy Hughes is an *authentic* pioneer.

Charles Chaplin — Looking over Chaplin's biography, his early beginnings did not indicate any possibility of the success that he lived as an actor, film director, producer and writer. His life started off on a sad note. His childhood and family life were filled with many hardships. The story of his experience with poverty and the lack of an education are heartbreaking. On a lighter side, it was said that Chaplin got a taste of show business at an early age when his parents had a short lived show business act. However, his family fell apart and he was left to support himself. He worked numerous jobs to survive, yet he never lost sight of his desire to become an actor one day. He did not allow his defeating start to be his finish. Surely the voices in his ears constantly reminded him that he was poor, uneducated and had no life. But nothing could stop him from dreaming his dreams; not even hardships. To his credit, Chaplin became one of the world's most celebrated actor and director. In one article he reflected on his change in fortunes; Sir Charles Chaplin said, *"What had happened? It seemed the world had suddenly changed, and had taken me into its fond embrace and adopted me."* As the Lord said to the Prophet Habakkuk, *"For the vision is yet for an appointed time, but at the end it shall speak, and not lie: though it tarry, wait for it; because it will surely come, it will not tarry.* ~ (Habakkuk 2:3, KJV)

Your mission. — It's important that you take time and prepare for your life's plans. If you are writing a book then spend time preparing and gathering information for your manuscript; if you are starting a business then attend network functions (with other business owners); if you're looking for romance —become the person you would like to meet (don't look for more than you are willing to give or be). You have a big life; it takes all of you to prepare for it. The U.S. Army (1980-2001) used the slogan, *Be All (That) You Can Be.* After 2001, the slogan changed to *Army Strong.* Taking the lead from the Army; not only should you "Be all that you can be", but you should also be "*authentic*-strong". Your heart, mind, will, love and focus must keep on living to fight for your life's purpose. Like the saying, *Uncle Sam wants you!* Life wants you to stop putting off the dream, sign-up, and live your *authentic* dreams. *"We proved that we are still a people capable of doing big things and tackling our biggest challenges."* ~Barack Obama

Wall of Thanks

Chapter 18:

As I walk in my *authentic* calling and experience: a brand new me evolving daily, exciting opportunities are being presented, further adventures, and I'm embracing more dreams … I am so thankful for family and friends. I wake-up each morning with a fresh cup of appreciation.

The publishing of *Your Authentic Self* is because of you. The people highlighted in this book gave their support in so many ways during my first publication. The encouragement received from the first book was the motivation — as the Staple Singers vocalized, *Let's Do it Again:*

I thank God (for my *authentic* life); my husband Clyde (for his love and support); my siblings Melvin (Judy), Calvin (Joyce), Aaron (Regina) and Jean (remember that our parents taught us to be *authentic* on the farm). Thanks to my wonderful nieces and nephews for their heartfelt support. Thanks to my extended family: the Bryants, Holmes, Dixons and Terrys.

9 781452 579436

I will never forget the special support of my wonderful "Fabulous Over Forty" family, giving special thanks to Gwen T., Angela R., Betty H., Belinda, Robin and Pam for being there with me and with so much love and service at my mother's home-going. Angela E., Janice, Laura S., Rich, Diane, Betsy, Isy, Girdine, Bettye A., Revette, Glenda, Laura M., Arjean, Jackie, Karen, Ayodele and Cynthia thanks for helping me with the support of the FO40. My fabulous guys: G. Fabre (always dependable), Jeff and Ed (the reality show is still possible), Terry (remember videos never forget), my photographer Shawn (thanks for the motivation), Ken, Paul "OCK" and Hassain thank you!

Supporters and friends: Much love to Adrienne, my high school teacher Mr. Richardson and Milton and Oniece for sharing your music and poetry with me; Minister Lee and Pat, Gail, Elizabeth, Stephanie, Evelyn and Danny (you are Attractive Bodies forever); Bob W., Valya, Beverly W., and Tim M.

Thank you for your donations and support to the FO40 projects: Johnny and Vondala, Avery, Chang, and Patricia.

Thanks for the speaking engagements: Gabrielle (Flat Shoals Librarian), Juanita (Fulton Cty. Librarian), Dr. S. Henry and Judy N. (North Clayton High School), Delores, Sharon "Ladee Storem", Trania Jones (Silver Lining), Drs.

Jonathon and Sylvia Carter (Siloam Int'l.), Drs. Charles and Georgia Davis (BBC) and Dr. Barbara King (Hillside International – and your grandson, James). To Loretta Howell and Judy G. thank you too for the speaking engagements.

My hometown - Woodbury, Georgia, supporters: to Pastor J.D. Walker (and family), Juanita and Scott, Annette, Vera and to every member of Mt. Pleasant Baptist Church - much love; to Bishop Thomas and Pastor Bobbie Daniels (Woodbury Miracle Center), Rev. Edward Harris and family, thank you for your love and support.

My fabulous neighbors: Teresa, Paige, Mae, Linda, Mrs. Blue, Robert, Rhonda, Bonnie and thank you to my other neighbors.

My prayer partners Esther (Larry, Ken & Renzie), Pastor Gibbs, Apostle Lewis and Pastor Poole ... much love.

Thank you Jennifer for the opportunity to be on WATC 57, to Kim for a great interview (and to other hosts and the staff at station); Penny and Iris (thank you for sharing my first book with so many) and to La'Kerri, thank you for your labor of love and time you gave to me in finishing this book.

Thank for the encouraging words and support: Shelia (SRT Realty), Rhonda (Dreamy Cupcakes), Mr. Greene (Air Force HVAC), Jonathan (Champion Supplies) and Phyllis (RPM).

My Clayton County supporters: Mayor Evelyn Wynn-Dixon, Ms. Emogene, Bob, Joan, Wendy (One on One) and Marie (M&M Braiding).

To my dear friends: Sharon C. (thank you Alvin for allowing me to use so much of your wife's time to finish this book), Christy, Linda, Beverly, Veverly and Faye J. thanks for your faith in me. Classmates: Arneatha (thank you Herbert for allowing me to also use some much of your wife's time to finish this book), Dorothy, Gwen, Josephine, Roger, Lawrence and Curtis. To the Balboa Press Staff – I'm so happy to be in the family.

As this book starts its *authentic* journey, for which it was called, I say, Farewell (suddenly) to my dear friend and supporter Rick and my 23 year old nephew Stevie. They were *authentic*.

CPSIA information can be obtained
at www.ICGtesting.com
Printed in the USA
FFOW04n0154240315
12115FF